Produktion und Logistik

Diese Reihe dient der Veröffentlichung neuer Forschungsergebnisse auf den Gebieten der Produktion und Logistik. Aufgenommen werden vor allem herausragende quantitativ orientierte Dissertationen und Habilitationsschriften. Die Publikationen vermitteln innovative Beiträge zur Lösung praktischer Anwendungsprobleme der Produktion und Logistik unter Einsatz quantitativer Methoden und moderner Informationstechnologie.

Kontakt

Professor Dr. Hans-Otto Günther
Technische Universität Berlin
H 95, Straße des 17. Juni 135
10623 Berlin

Volker Windeck

A Liner Shipping Network Design

Routing and Scheduling Considering Environmental Influences

Foreword by Prof. Dr. Hartmut Stadtler

Springer Gabler

Volker Windeck
Hamburg, Germany

Dissertation University of Hamburg, 2012

ISBN 978-3-658-00698-3 ISBN 978-3-658-00699-0 (eBook)
DOI 10.1007/978-3-658-00699-0

The Deutsche Nationalbibliothek lists this publication in the Deutsche Nationalbibliografie; detailed bibliographic data are available in the Internet at http://dnb.d-nb.de.

Library of Congress Control Number: 2012951488

Springer Gabler

Printed on acid-free paper

Springer Gabler is a brand of Springer DE.
Springer DE is part of Springer Science+Business Media.
www.springer-gabler.de

Foreword

Transport by ship is regarded as the most economical and ecological means of transport for carrying large and heavy volumes over long distances. Still or as a result, total world-wide container shipping is due to its mere size one of the largest carbon dioxide (CO2) and sulphur oxides (SOX) polluters today. Hence, recommendations for reducing these emissions are most welcome.

This thesis not only presents a decision support system for designing a liner shipping network and its operation. It is also a nice example for how Operations Research models and algorithms can help to improve both economical and ecological objectives simultaneously!

This research is based on detailed real-world data for currents, winds and waves a ship may face on a given passage. It is used as an input to a shortest path and a strategic mathematical model. As means to reduce emissions and fuel consumption, slow steaming as well as additional propulsion systems are incorporated into the models. A large computational test with container ships equipped with the latest technology for an additional wind propulsion system (i.e., a kite) shows that significant reductions of fuel consumption can be expected only on specific passages (like the North Atlantic). Much more important in this respect is the choice of an appropriate speed (including slow steaming) for each leg on a ships round trip.

Although Volker Windeck has put much emphasis on making use of the latest and most accurate data, it is recommended not to generalize his findings on the potential reduction of fuel consumption and emissions. Instead, shipping companies should implement the model suite developed and documented in this thesis and perform their own calculations considering their fleet of container ships and customer base.

It has been a great pleasure to have been able to collaborate with Volker Windeck during the last four years and to see a fascinating topic ripening and yielding computational results which in this breadth could neither be achieved by simple human reasoning nor by real-word experiments.

I sincerely hope that his model suite including a highly innovative matheuristic will not only be of interest to the academic world but will also be used intensively by shipping companies.

Hartmut Stadtler

Preface

In this thesis the results of the research are presented which were carried out at the Institute for Logistics and Transportation of the University of Hamburg.

I am very grateful to Prof. Dr. Hartmut Stadtler for giving me the opportunity to engage in this research topic which is linked to very challenging, technical questions and contains a great portion of maritime flair, too. Whenever necessary he offered his time and always got me back on track with his enormous experience and stimulating suggestions.

Prof. Dr. Knut Haase deserves special thanks for reviewing my thesis as a co-supervisor and also providing valuable advice on how to solve my shortest path problem. Also, I thank Prof. Dr. Stefan Voß for taking on the chair on the dissertation committee and being an obviously interested reader of my dissertation which he expressed in enriching suggestions and questions during my thesis defence.

My thanks also to the core of in-house supporters and dear colleagues Christopher Haub, Florian Kröger and Julian Wulf for proofreading and multiple good suggestions and Sylvia Kilian and Stefanie Nonnsen for providing a friendly atmosphere. Much support was given from my former colleagues Dr. Martin Albrecht, Dr. Carolin Püttmann and Dr. Christian Seipl who were always offering their help to get me started with my research.

My sincere thanks go to all the companies and organizations, that offered me their time when discussing my research project. Among them Dr. Thomas Bruns and Mr. Heinz-G. Hill of the DWD (German Meteorological Service) who deserve a special thanks for their interest and support and especially providing me with weather data on wind and waves being a most valuable basis of my research.

Finally, I would like to thank my wife and family for accompanying me with unlimited love and support, which allowed me to accomplish this set goal.

Volker Windeck

Contents

List of Figures

List of Tables

Abbreviations

DWD	Deutscher Wetterdienst, governmental German weather service
dwt	Deadweight tonnage, ship carrying capacity measured in metric tons
GMES	Global Monitoring for Environment and Security
HFO	Heavy Fuel Oil
IMO	International Maritime Organisation
ITTC	International Towing Tank Conference
LFCP	Least Fuel Consumption Problem
LNG	Liquefied natural gas
LTA	Latest Time of Arrival
MIP-model	Mixed Integer Programming Model
MPLSFP	Multi-Period Liner Ship Fleet Planning Problem
MTTP	Minimum Travel Time Problem
NG	Natural Gas
NOX	Nitrogen Oxides
OD	OD
PDP	Pick-up and Delivery Problem
Ro-Ro	Roll-on-Roll-off
SDNP	Service Network Design Problem
SOX	sulphur oxides
SPP	Shortest Path Problem
SPPRC	Shortest Path Problems with Resource Constraints
SPPTW	Shortest Path Problem with Time Window Constraints
TEU	20 feet equivalent unit
TSP	Travelling Salesman Problem
TW	Time Window

UAVs	Unmanned Aerial Vehicles
VNS	Variable Neighbourhood Search
VRP	Vehicle Routing Problem

Nomenclature

α_W	Angle between true and apparent wind
α_{CU}	Angle between direction of ocean current and ship's desired course
β_W	Angle between the true wind and the fair wind
Δ	Total travelled distance of one round trip
η_D	Efficiency of propulsion
η_S	Efficiency of transmission
γ_P	Pitch angle of flying kite
γ_W	Incidence angle between apparent wind and ships' direction
γ_{AW}	Wind direction of apparent wind
∇	Displacement of a ship
ν	Kinematic viscosity
ρ_A	Density of air
ρ_{SW}	Density of sea water (SW)
ζ	Wave height
a_i	Earliest arrival time at network point i
A_K	Size of kite
a_k	Ship type k dependent coefficient for the fuel consumption formula
A_S	Wetted surface area of a ships hull
A_{AWS}	Above water surface of a ship
B	Breadth of a ship
b_i	Latest arrival time at network point i
b_k	Ship type k dependent coefficient for the fuel consumption formula
C	Centre point of SPP network
C_∇	Ship's volume-length coefficient
C_F	Friction coefficient
C_i^p	Fuel consumed when reaching network point i on path p

C_M	main frame surface area
C_P	Ship's prismatic coefficient
C_R	Remaining drag coefficient
C_T	Total drag coefficient
c_W	Kite wind resistance coefficient
$C_{\pm i}$	Additional centre points along a line through centre point C
$C_{B,AYRE}$	Ship's Ayre block coefficient
$C_{I1,I2}$	Course between two interception points I_1 and I_2
c_{ij}	Costs arising when traversing on an arc between two network points i and j
CO_2	Carbon dioxide
D_c^{GC}	Great circle distance between cargo c's loading and unloading harbour
$D_{I1,I2}$	Great circle distance measured in degree between interception points I_1 and I_2
D_{I_1,I_2}	Distance between interception points I_1 and I_2
D_{sek}	Denotes the two turning point harbours s and e for each ship type k
EC_{nor}	original, normal energy consumption
EC_{red}	specific energy consumption at reduced speed
F	Visiting frequency
F_N	Froude's number
g	Earth's gravity
I_i	Interception points of a network arc
k_{yy}	Longitudinal radius of gyration about an axis through the centre of gravity
L	Length of a ship
L_i	Label storing all information of network point i within a label-setting algorithm
LCB	Longitudinal position of centre of buoyancy from midships
N_1, N_2	Origin and destination points of a network arc
N_H	Number of visited harbours
N_S	Number of ships needed to uphold a promised visiting frequency
P_B	Braking power
P_i^p	Set of paths to reach node i indexed by p
$pred(L)$	Predecessor node of a label
R_G	Gross resistance, combination of all resistances
R_G	Sum of all ship resistances
R_K	Kite propulsion force

R_T	Calm water resistance
R_W	Wind resistance
$R_{KD}(\gamma_{AW})$	Apparent wind direction dependent kite propulsion force component
R_{KV}	Kite propulsion force
$R_{KV}(V_{AW})$	Apparent wind velocity dependent kite propulsion force component
$R_{sea,K}$	Additional wave resistance as proposed by Kreitner (1939)
$R_{sea,MM}$	Dimensionless additional wave resistance according to Moor and Murdy (1968)
Re	Reynolds number
T	Draught of a ship
T_H	Average time spent in harbour for loading and unloading activities
T_i^p	Needed travel time to reach network point i on path p
t_{ij}	Travel time needed when traversing on an arc between two network points i and j
tt_{ijk}	Travel time, a ship of type k needs to travel from harbour i to harbour j
V	Average fleet speed
v_p	Speed taken within a label-setting algorithm on path p
V_s	Ship speed
V_{AW}	Wind velocity of apparent wind
V_{CO}	Velocity of a ship over ground in course direction
V_{CU}	Ocean current velocity
V_{FW}	Fair wind
V_{nor}	original, normal speed setting
V_{red}	reduced speed
V_{TW}	True wind
V_T	Tip velocity
a, b, c, d	Parameters for estimating apparent wind direction dependent kite force
g	Gram
kg	Kilogram
km	Kilometre
kn	Speed in knots
lat	Latitude of a a coordinate
lon	Longitude of a coordinate
nm	Nautical mile
t	Metric ton

Parameters and Random Variables

β	Progressing time between two consecutive service arcs
$\overline{inv_i}$	Upper bound on inventory level of LNG in harbour i
$\overline{tw_i}, \underline{tw_i}$	Time interval for each harbour and cargo combination i
$\overline{u_{dij}}$	Upper bound on passenger flow on an arc connecting harbours i and j
$\overline{u_{ij}}$	Upper bound on ferry flow on an arc connecting harbours i and j
$\underline{inv_i}$	Lower bound on inventory level of LNG in harbour i
$\underline{v_k}; \overline{v_k}$	Given minimum and maximum speed a ship of type k can travel at
c_{ijk}	Cost for traversing an arc from harbour i to j for a ship of type k
c_{ij}	Costs for operating a trip between harbours i and j
cap	Ferry capacity
cap_k	Capacity of a ship of type k
cap_{ijk}	Capacity of a ship of type k when travelling from harbour i to harbour j
cf	Fixed costs for hiring or owning a ferry per day
$charter_k$	Daily charter-rates representing the fixed costs to operate a ship of type k for one day
$costs_{ijkv}$	Speed dependent variable travel costs for a ship of type k when travelling directly from harbour i to j
cp_{it}	Costs for producing LNG in harbour i and time period t
ct_{kr}	Costs for a ship of type k travelling on route r
d_i	Demand at harbour i
d_{di}	Passenger demand of origin destination pair d for harbours $i \in N_d$
$demand_c$	Weekly amount of cargo c in TEU
$demand_{ij}$	Expected amount of container available for transportation from their origin harbour i to destination harbour j
f	Maximum amount of ferries
h_i	Harbour visiting indicator has value 1 for delivery harbours and -1 for pick-up harbours i
l_{iktr}	Number of tanks unloaded from ship of type k at harbour i in t on route r
$loadH_c$	Loading harbour of cargo c
lta_j	Latest arrival time at harbour j
m	Sufficiently large number

$ncap_i$	Number of ships that can unload simultaneously in harbour i
p_j	Pick-up load to be picked up in harbour j
p_{it}	Upper bound on production of LNG in harbour i and time period t
q_k	Capacity of a ship of type k
q_{iktr}	(Un-)Loading volume at harbour i by a ship of type k in time period t on route r
qc_i	Weight of cargo from harbour i
rev_c	Revenue per TEU for transporting cargo c
rev_d^c	Revenue for origin destination pair d
rev_i^h	Revenue for loading cargo from harbour i
rev_{ij}	Revenue obtained from transporting a container from its origin i to its destination harbour j
rev_{it}^g	Revenue obtained from transporting and selling gas in harbour i and time period t
s_{ik}	Necessary time to service harbour i by a ship of type k
s_{it}^{LNG}	Lower bound on sales of LNG in harbour i and time period t
t_c^{max}	Allowed maximum transportation time of cargo c
t_k	Availability of a ship of type k measured in days
t_{ijk}	Time for traversing an arc from harbour i to j by a ship of type k
t_{ij}	Travel time between harbour i and j
$tcap_k$	Maximum number of tanks in ship of type k
$tijt_{cdek}^{v^{min}}$	Total travel time between the loading harbour d and unloading harbours e of cargo c, for all four direction combinations, when travelling at slowest possible speed v^{min} on a ship of type k
tl_{ik}	Required loading and unloading time of a ship of type k in harbour i
$tload_{ck}$	loading time of cargo c on board of a ship of type k
tt_d	Travel time of origin destination pair d for direct service
tt_k^{max}	Maximum total travel time for a ship of type k
tt_{ijdkv}	Time a ship of type k needs when travelling from harbour i to j
$ttt_{i(c)d(i)j(c)d(j)k}^{max}$	Maximum allowed travel time of cargo c from its loading harbour $i(c)$ to its unloading harbour $j(c)$, which can either be on the inbound or outbound part of a round trip indicated by $d(i)$ and $d(j)$ for the loading and unloading

	harbour respectively
$tunload_{ck}$	unloading time of cargo c from board of a ship of type k
tv	Travel time value
$unloadH_c$	Unloading harbour of cargo c
w_k	Number of tanks on ship k
wv	Waiting time value
x_{ijktr}	1, if a ship of type k (un-)loads at harbour i in t before travelling to harbour j on route r; 0, otherwise
z_{iktr}	1, if ship k visits harbour i in t on route r; 0, otherwise

Indices, Sets and Index Sets

0	Depot, mainland harbour
$c \in C$	Cargo
$CargoRoute_{hdk}$	Set of all cargoes $(c, d(i), d(j))$ that stay on board of a ship of type k when passing harbour h in direction d)
$d \in R$	Set of origin and destination pairs
D_d	Destination arcs of the passenger network
$DirL_{cdekghf}$	All direct connections $d \in D$, $(g, h) \in H$ on the partial-trip from a cargo's loading harbour d_i to its unloading harbour d_j, where a ship of type k can transport cargo c
$e, d \in D$	Outbound or inbound direction of round trip
$e, h, i, j, e, s \in H$	Harbour index
$H_c \subset H_p$	Set of pick-up harbours for mandatory cargo
H_d	Set of delivery harbours
H_k	Cargo at set of Harbours, corresponding to cargo a ship of type k can load
$H_o \subset H_p$	Set of pick-up harbours for optional cargo
H_p	Set of pick-up harbours
$H_{pk}; H_{dk}$	Set of all pick-up and delivery harbours for cargo a ship of type k can load
$k \in K$	Set of ship types
$Load_i$	Set of cargoes c, that can be picked up in harbour i
N, A	Set of nodes and arcs for the ferry network
$N^b, N^e \subset N$	Set of nodes at the beginning and ending of the planning interval
N^D	Set of delivery harbours
N^P	Set of pick-up harbours
N_d, A_d	Set of nodes and arcs for the passenger network
O_d	Origin arcs of the passenger network
$o_k; d_k$	Origin and destination of a ship of type k, either harbour

	or artificial position at sea
$r \in R_k$	Set of routes for ships of type k
S, S_d	Set of service arcs for the ferry and passenger network
$t \in T$	Set of time periods
$Unload_i$	Set of all cargoes that can be unloaded in harbour i
$v \in V$	Set of possible average speed settings between two harbours
W, W_d	Set of waiting arcs for the ferry and passenger network

Variables

Λ_{kr}	Number of round trips a ship of type k makes on its assigned route r during one planning interval
A_i	Arrival time at harbour i
D_{sek}	1, if s and e are turning point harbours for ship of type k; 0, otherwise
H_{idk}	1, if harbour i is visited by a ship of type k either on the inbound (d=1) or outbound (d=2) part of the round trip; 0, otherwise
$Har_{(id)k}$	point in time when a ship of type k arrives at harbour i
$Hde_{(id)k}$	Point in time when a ship of type k leaves harbour i on the in- or outbound part of its round trip
L_{jk}	Cargo on board of a ship of type k after leaving harbour j
N_k	Number of round trips a ship of type k makes on its assigned route during one planning interval
$NShips_k$	Number of ships of type k that are needed to guarantee a weekly (every 168 h) visit to all visited harbours on the round trip
S_{it}	Inventory level of storage in harbour i in time period t
$Ship_k$	1, if a ship of type k is in use; 0, otherwise
$Slack_{idk}$	Either waiting time for a ship of type k lying in the roads at harbour i in direction d or time used for repairs and overhauls
TH^E_{jk}	1, if harbour j is the most easterly harbour of the round trip of a ship of type k; 0, otherwise
TH^W_{ik}	1, if harbour i is the most westerly harbour of the round trip of a ship of type k; 0 , otherwise
$TijT_{cdek}$	Lower bound of travel time for a ship of type k when transporting cargo c from its loading to its unloading harbour
TT_{ijk}	Travel time of the direct connection between harbours i and j for a ship of type k's round trip
V_{ijdkv}	1, if ships of type k are travelling with speed v from harbour

	i to j in direction d; 0, otherwise
V_{ijk}	Speed a ship of type k should travel at, when traversing on an arc from harbour i to harbour j
X_{dij}	Passenger flow in a time-space network of origin destination pair d
X_{ijdk}	1, if a ship of type k is travelling directly from harbour i to harbour j in direction d, without stopping at harbours that lie in between; 0, otherwise
X_{ijk}	1, if a ship of type k is traversing an arc from harbour i to j; 0, otherwise
Y_{cdk}	1, if cargo c is picked up on the inbound or outbound part d of the round trip of a ship of type k; 0, otherwise
Y_{ijk}	Number of cargo loaded in TEU by a ship of type k from an origin harbour i to a destination harbour j
Y_{ij}	Ferry flow in the ferry time-space network
Y_{it}	Sales or production of LNG in harbour i in time period t
$Z_{cd(i)d(j)k}$	1, if cargo c is picked up at its origin harbour i and dropped off at its destination harbour j on either the inbound or outbound trip $(d(i), d(j))$ of a ship of type k's round trip; 0, otherwise

Chapter 1

Introduction

1.1 Motivation

Both, reductions of costs as well as emissions are driving shipping companies to operate their fleet in slow steaming mode. In this thesis a strategic liner shipping network design decision support system is presented, which takes three environmental influences into account: waves, ocean currents and wind. The developed models will show the impact of environmental influences and the use of additional propulsion systems on the cost structure or the on-time delivery of a liner shipping network and its schedule. We will present a Matheuristic based on a Variable Neighbourhood solution approach, that can solve the corresponding optimization problem in reasonable computational time.

Growing ecological concerns have an influence on fleet size and speed selection. Two different sides put pressure on ship operators to reduce emissions. On the one side, governments are driven by the IMO (International Maritime Organisation) to force ships to use marine diesel fuel that emits less NOX (nitrogen oxides) and SOX (sulphur oxides). Due to its higher quality this marine diesel is sold at a higher price than regular bunker fuel according to the MARPOL Annex VI (International Convention for the Prevention of Marine Pollution from Ships). On the other side companies (e.g. Tchibo, a German coffee shop chain also offering other goods such as clothing, household items and electronics) intend to reduce emissions, when shipping their goods (Tchibo 2009). Due to the fact that these items are mainly produced in East Asia and therefore transported by ship to Europe, a large amount of the emissions will be generated by sea transport. Besides using fuel that emits less NOX and SOX, reducing the speed of ships can reduce emissions even more, because fuel consumption increases with speed almost to the power of three.

Increasing fuel costs and growing ecological concerns are forcing ship owners and operators as well as forwarding companies to operate their fleet in a so called slow steaming mode. The tremendous rise of bunker fuel costs (over 28% in the last 12 months; BWI 2011) now represents an increasing portion of freight charges. To reduce bunker fuel costs per trip, operators can decrease their fleets average speed, resulting in reduced fuel consumption. Because ship operators guarantee harbour visits at a fixed frequency, the increase in travel time due to the slower speed can lead to a need for additional ships. The majority of liner shipping companies presently ensures harbour visits at a weekly frequency.

Other approaches to reduce fuel consumption or sulphur emission rely on using alternative propulsion techniques. Recent ideas include the use of solar power, wave propelled ships or wind dependent propulsion systems. Wind propulsion systems are the most practical and advanced techniques. The system we consider in this thesis is a kite system like the one manufactured by SkySails (SkySails 2011). Depending on the wind direction and speed, in relation to the ships direction and speed, these kites can lower the engine power output when travelling at a given speed and thus reduce fuel consumption. Other alternative propulsion techniques use the effect of Flettner rotors (e.g. E-Ship, Enercon 2010).

Depending on the vessel operator's perspective the models presented in this thesis can be used as a decision support to find the combination of optimal routes of a ship within a given fleet or calculate the expected savings by using alternative propulsion modes can be calculated. The decision of investing into an alternative propulsion technique can be one of the results found with this decision support system. In essence, significant savings in costs, fuel or emissions can be expected when using the decision support system presented in this thesis.

1.2 Outline

The remainder of this thesis is organized as follows. In Chapter 2 basic knowledge on maritime transportation is provided with its special needs and conditions in comparison to other modes of transportation. Subsequently some definitions that provide the reader with a common understanding of terms used are given.

One of the tasks of this thesis is to find an optimal route (concerning time, cost, fuel consumption and speed) between two coordinates (i.e. two harbours). At the operational planning level an optimal route is calculated by taking environmental influences such as wind, currents and waves into account. Additionally, the benefit of alternative propulsion technologies, such as the kite system described, are analysed.

We find that the results of the operational, environmental routing has a significant influence on the design of a liner network. As an example, ships operate on more northerly routes during summer months than in winter months. Poor weather conditions results in higher consumption of fuel and therefore a change of routes between summer and winter months is recommended.

For the operational planning level we construct a grid network consisting of nodes which represent a point on the way from one harbour to another. A cell within this network cornered by four nodes represents a field of identical weather conditions. These weather conditions include:

- wind force
- wind direction
- wave height
- wave period of appearance
- wave direction
- ocean current strength
- ocean current direction

Based on this network we obtain the cost and time minimal route by using an extended label-setting algorithm based on Dijkstra's-Algorithm (Dijkstra 1959). The operational, environmental routing is dealt with in Chapter 3.

Based on this operational planning problem is a strategic planning task, that finds the optimal network and fleet size, operating in a liner shipping service. A typical example of those vessels are container ships. The strategic network design, indicating which ship types should use a specific schedule to fulfil all harbour's load demand is generated by a Matheuristic. For a set of possible harbours of call with a given amount of demand we generate a solution that gives the number of ships and travel times between all harbours that should be visited by a given set of ship types. The strategic network design model is presented in Chapter 4.

The effects on the design of a liner shipping network for ships travelling with and without a wind driven additional propulsion system is shown by numerical tests (Chapter 5). Even for ships operating on a liner service without additional propulsion systems, we will determine the impact of considering environmental and speed dependent costs between two consecutive harbours.

In Chapter 6 the thesis is concluded with a summary and an outlook.

Chapter 2

Maritime Transportation

The aim of this chapter is to introduce the reader to maritime transportation. In the following a short overview on numbers and figures of world trade, ocean going transportation and especially container ship transportation, which is the focus of this thesis, is given.

About 90% of world trade, in terms of volume, is transported on ocean going ships, which makes up 70% of world trade in terms of value (see Hoffmann 2008, p. 14). Within maritime transportation, ocean going ships can be mainly classified into bulk carrier which transport dry bulk products, tankers, carrying for example liquefied gas or crude oil, container ships, general cargo transporting ships and passenger ships. In terms of carrying capacity in tons, the majority of cargo can be transported by tankers with a share of 41.77% or 475.8 mil. dwt (deadweight tonnage, the ship carrying capacity measured in metric tons) followed by bulk carriers and container ships with 36.63% (417.2 mil. dwt) and 13.28% (151.3 mil. dwt) respectively. General cargo carrying ships account for 7.85% (89.4 mil. dwt) and passenger ships only for 0.48% (5.5 mil. dwt) (ISL 2011a, p. IV). In terms of value these figures slightly change because consumer goods have a high ratio of value per ton and are almost exclusivley transported by container (Stopford 2009, see p. 505 and 518). This makes container ship transportation the most important mode of ocean going transportation.

Figure 2.1 shows the yearly container handling for different regions of the world. Note, that between the years 2000 and 2008 the worldwide container handling activities have increased steadily. Only for the years 2001 and 2008 the annual growth rate was below 10%. With the beginning of the financial crisis in 2008 maritime container transportation dropped and finally in 2009, the container handling activities decreased by 8.9%. But in the future the annual growth rate is expected to rise by 10% or more. Latest figures state that the growth for the year 2010 was nearly 13% (ISL 2011b, p. 5).

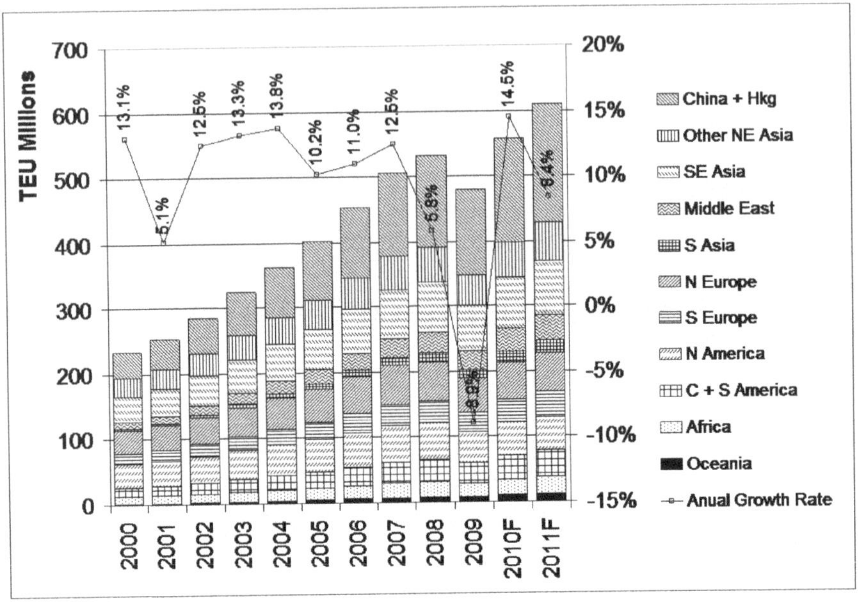

Figure 2.1: Global container handling from 2000 to 2009 and forecasts for 2010 and 2011, according to Tiedemann (2011)

In regard to regional growth of container handling activities, all regions show an increase in container handling activities for the years 2000 to 2011. Again only in the year 2009 all regions had a cutback in container handling activities. The growth rates for China and Hong Kong are the highest, followed by South East Asia.

The amount of container ships and their average container carrying capacity has been increasing steadily over the years. In the last 20 years the average carrying capacity of container ships increased from 1,250 TEU (twenty feet equivilant units) in 1990 to 2,880 TEU at the beginning of 2011 (ISL 2011b, p. 13). The Hamburg Index for Containership time-charter rates, classifies container ships into 9 different classes. Gearless ships are divided into three classes of 200 – 299 TEU, 300 – 500 TEU and 2,000 – 2,999 TEU carrying capacity. The other 6 classes of geared ships have carrying capacities between 200 and 1,999 TEU. The Hamburg Index is measured in dollars per 14-ton slot and day. 14 tons is the average weight of a loaded twenty feet container and therefore a slot is comparable to 1 TEU. This index shows decreasing charter rates for container ships beginning in the year 2008 and is only slowly increasing again in recent months. Since the development of charter rates is similar for all of the different container ship classes, only the gearless ship class with a carrying capacity of 2,000 – 2,999 TEU will be regarded as a representative for the charter rate development of all ship classes. Charter rates for this class fell from above 18 $ in year 2005 down to around 13 $ in 2008 and further down to only 2.1 $ in 2009. From then on, the prices slowly increased up to 6.2 $ in 2010 (ISL 2011a, p. 158). This shows, that charter rates for container ships have not fully recovered back to the pre-financial crisis level. A similar development can be seen for freight rates in the major liner trade routes where as an example, prices for containers transported between Asia and Europe fell from 1,837 $ per TEU in the third quarter of 2008 down to 897 $ per TEU in the second quarter of 2009 and have slowly increased to 1,422 $ per TEU in the fourth quarter of 2009 (Asariotis et al. 2011, p. 88).

Bunker fuel prices have a great impact on the development of the worldwide maritime transportation business and have been subject to change parallel to the world economic development. Due to the growing world economy and subsequently increasing transportation demand, oil and gas prices rose steeply before the financial crisis in 2008. In July 2008 bunker fuel (CST 180) was sold at 720 US $/MT in european harbours (average price for harbours Hamburg, Rotterdam and Le Havre) but dropped down to 236 $/MT in December 2008, the hight of the financial crisis. After that prices again steadily increased up to a new all time high of 735 $/MT in April 2011 (ISL 2011b, p. 74).

These statistics only show some of the many influencing parameters on maritime transportation and especially container shipping. To be able to quickly adapt to changing environments, decision support systems are needed, that account for as many of these interacting parameters as possible. Decision makers are then able to quickly reorganise their business based on those plans received with the objective to improve economic competitiveness.

2.1 Freight Transporation Systems

Generally transportation systems can be subdivided into land-based and water-based transportation or transportation by air. In the following we will only concentrate on freight transportation and not on passenger transportation. In many areas transportation systems compete for cargo but differ in transportation costs, capacity, speed, on time delivery, and the density of their network.

Road based transportation which is normally performed for example by trucks is more flexible and can operate in many areas. The network is very dense for most populated regions and costs for loading and unloading facilities and equipment are very low compared to other modes of transportation. Predominant restrictions for trucks are the relatively small capacity in regard to volume and weight. Additionally, governmental regulations on wheel times reduce the benefits of using this mode of transportation. A truck is, other than for example a ship, in almost all cases not operated around the clock. There is usually only one driver per truck, so that the truck will not be operated, when the driver has to have a mandatory rest period. On the other hand, trucks are especially cost and time effective for transporting individually packaged goods over short to medium distances. The advantage of water-based transportation is the ability of shipping bulk cargo and large volume cargo over long distances. With increasing distances trucks loose their advantage in favour of rail road transportation. In comparison to trucks a train has a more limited network to travel on, but is more energy efficient and therefore also more environmental friendly. The advantage of trains is the fast transportation of bulk cargo on long distances. The disadvantages are longer stops and cargo handling costs.

The fastest mode of transportation is by aircraft, on which mainly high priced goods with a high ratio of price to volume or weight are transported. As expected, the higher speed implies higher transportation costs. However, a higher speed is usually only achieved on longer distances. On short distances cargo handling times would add up to higher transportation times in total compared to trucks or trains for instance.

A lot slower but a cheaper mode of transportation than trucks, trains and aircrafts are ships. We distinguish between inland or river barges and ocean going ships. Where inland or river barges mainly compete with trucks and trains, in many cases, the only alternative to ocean going ships are aircrafts. For example, cargo can only be transported between Europe and Northern America or Asia and Northern America by ship or aircraft. Between Europe and Asia, cargo might be shipped by ocean going ships, aircraft or even by train via Russia. In the following, when mentioning ships, we will only consider ocean going ships. Even though there is a high potential for further decreasing emissions, ships are known to be environmentally friendly in comparison with other modes of transportation. The only drawbacks are that ships travel a lot slower than other vehicles and that they are restricted to harbours where they can load or unload cargo.

Christiansen et al. (2007, p. 192) compare many different characteristics of five different modes of transportation (see Table 2.1).

Operational characteristic	Mode				
	Ships	Aircraft	Truck	Train	Pipeline
Barriers to entry	small	medium	small	large	large
Industry concentration	low	medium	low	high	high
Fleet variety (physical & economic)	large	small	small	small	NA
Power unit is an integral part of the transportation unit	yes	yes	often	no	NA
Transportation unit size	fixed	fixed	usually fixed	variable	NA
Operating around the clock	usually	seldom	seldom	usually	usually
Trip (or voyage) length	days-weeks	hours-days	hours-days	hours-days	days-weeks
Operational uncertainty	larger	larger	smaller	smaller	smaller
Right of way	shared	shared	shared	dedicated	dedicated
Pays harbour fees	yes	yes	no	no	no
Route tolls	possible	none	possible	possible	possible
Destination change while underway	possible	no	no	no	possible
Harbour period spans multiple operational time windows	yes	no	no	yes	NA
Vessel-harbour compatibility depends on load weight	yes	seldom	no	no	NA
Multiple products shipped together	yes	no	yes	yes	NA
Returns to origin	no	no	yes	no	NA

NA – not applicable

Table 2.1: Comparison of operational characteristics of freight transportation modes (Christiansen et al. 2007, p 192)

Other than trucks and trains, ships usually have to pay a harbour fee and stay in a harbour for multiple operational time periods during loading and unloading operations. Additionally the amount of cargo loaded on board of a ship may decide on whether that ship can enter a harbour or not, due to its cargo weight dependent draught. Furthermore, weather and tides sometimes may restrict the call at a harbour. In many cases ships are travelling in international waters, which again leads, compared to trucks and trains, to higher operational uncertainties.

Despite their fundamental differences, ships and aircraft have much in common. Both are highly dependent on technological and economical developments and are to a great extent subject to weather uncertainties. The fixed size of the vehicles and their independence of a central depot are problems in common. With truck transportation the volume and carrying capacity can be changed by simply attaching a trailer. Differences can be seen in the way these two types of vehicles operate. A great portion of the air traffic is a combination of cargo and passenger transportation, where cargo is transported in an aircraft's belly. Since passengers preferably travel by day, this combined transportation usually takes place during daytime hours, whereas ships are operated 24 hours a day.

Finally, ships differ from all other transportation vehicles in their high diversity. In most cases ships are built unique. Only very few classes of ships are built in small series. Aircrafts vary only between a small amount of aircraft types, whereas the size of a truck is very much limited due to road restrictions in terms of hight, breadth, and weight. Therefore, only a couple of standard sizes have become accepted. Compared to trucks, rail road wagons have similar sizes but a whole train can vary in length. The shorter a train is, the less efficient its operation is. The total length of a train is limited by the total weight a rail road engine can pull, judicial restrictions and operational restrictions, like the maximum length of a rail way station.

In the shipping industry, ships are classified by their designated use. Bulk cargoes appear in liquid and dry shape. Tankers for example are built to transport liquids in bulk. Best known are crude oil tankers or liquefied gas tankers. The so called bulk carriers are designed to transport dry bulk, like iron ore or coal. Roll-on-Roll-off (Ro-Ro) ships are designed to allow cars and trucks to enter the ship via a ramp. Refrigerated ships are able to transport perishable goods. Bananas are a classical example, on long distances. Instead of transporting these goods on especially designed ships for transport of refrigerated freight on long distances, many perishable goods are nowadays being transported in reefers (refrigerated containers) on container ships. For this type of container, container ships need to have special storing positions with plugs for the electric power supply of the reefer containers.

On the other side general cargo ships are capable of transporting all kinds of cargo. These cargoes usually have a special size and must be handled separately. These ships often have on-board cranes for loading and unloading. The loading and unloading of this kind of cargo is in most cases very time and labour intensive. Other types of ships are ferries, cruise ships, naval and fishing ships. This thesis purely concentrates on container ships, which transport either standardized 20 feet or 40 feet containers. Containers are counted in 20 feet equivalent units (TEU), so that a 40 feet container counts for 2 TEU. The maximum load capacity of a TEU is 28 tons at a maximum volume of 1,000 cubic feet of volume (see Christiansen et al. 2007, p. 199).

2.2 Terms and Definitions

Ronen (1983) introduced a classification scheme for routing and scheduling problems in maritime transportation according to Lawrence (1972) where planning tasks are divided into industrial-, tramp- and liner-shipping problems.

Liner shipping operations can be compared to a bus line service. A characteristic of these maritime pick-up and delivery problems is that ships never return to a depot and proceed to operate on their assigned route according to a published schedule. Additionally, harbours within a single circling liner service might be called at more than once by the same ship, which is not solvable with standard routing models of land-based transportation (see Page 20).

Tramp shipping is comparable to a taxi service. Mainly spot cargo or project cargo is loaded as a full ship load at a specific harbour and delivered to the cargo's destination harbour. Where spot cargo is cargo that is picked up on a short term basis, and other than cargo a shipping company is obliged to transport under long-term contracts, can optionally been transported if capacity is still available on ships. Cargo of extraordinary size, like machines and larger vehicles, is referred to as project cargo. After delivery of the cargo, the tramp ship might have to travel empty to another harbour before loading the next cargo according to the next order.

Whereas in liner and tramp shipping the objective is to maximize profit, the aim in **industrial shipping** is to minimize costs. Usually ships operating in industrial mode are controlled by the owner of the cargo. These ships are often scheduled to operate according to the needs of a closed supply chain and have a vital part in the system.

When discussing maritime transportation planning problems, we always refer to water-side planning tasks. Land-side planning tasks, such as ship berth allocation and crane scheduling, container yard or ship management, are not discussed in detail in this thesis.

To further distinguish planning problems of maritime transportation, a distinction between strategic, tactical and operational problems will be made. Strategic problems are those with a longer planning horizon compared to tactical and operational problems.

Christiansen et al. (2007) assign

- market and trade selection,
- ship design,
- network and transportation system design,
- decisions for fleet size and mix
- harbour or terminal location, size and design

to the strategic planning problems.

Market and trade selections are understood as the shipping companies decision of which countries and regions and therefore markets to take into consideration for a harbour visit of its ships. In regard to container liner shipping this decision will be, which harbours of a specific liner service should be visited on a regular basis and which harbours should not be visited because no additional profit is expected.

Questions of a ship design problem might be the dimensions of a ship, length, breadth, draught and cargo holding capacity, a ship's service speed and therefore engine size and its transportation purpose. This decision has an impact on the harbours it can visit and the routes it can travel on. The draught of a ship might prevent a ship from entering a too shallow harbour and the length, breadth and draught of a ship might not allow for a canal passage. The maximum size of the panama canal locks is a threshold according to which ships are classified in panamax or post-panamax ships. Ships with post-panamax size cannot travel through the Panama Canal due to their size. Bigger ships like capesize ships are even too big to enter the larger Suez Canal and therefore have to travel around the Cape of Good Hope, the most southerly point of Africa.

A maritime network and transportation system design determines the harbours one or multiple ships of the same or different type are visiting according to their transportation task. This also includes the decision, which harbour to declare to operate as a transshipment harbour in a liner network environment.

Most of the published decision support systems for solving maritime transportation problems cover more than one of the above mentioned strategical planning problems. As will be shown later, solution approaches might spread across strategic and tactical problems or technical and operational problems. As an example the fleet size and mix decision problem which specifies the type, size and number of ships, is often solved in combination with a network and transportation system design. In this thesis the harbour or terminal location size and design will not be examined. In our strategic approach several harbours will be considered but will not have to necessarily be visited by a liner service. This thesis will determine the maximum profit generated and the specific number and type of ships, that can operate on developed liner round trips and schedules while transporting assigned cargo. The resulting combination of fleet size and mix, routing and scheduling and cargo assignment problem is classified as a strategic decision support system for this thesis.

Tactical planning problems in maritime transportation according to Christiansen et al. (2007) are again the

- adjustment of the size and mix of the fleet,
- fleet deployment,
- ship routing and scheduling and
- inventory ship routing

The fleet deployment task answers the question, which ships to assign to liner services or when thinking of industrial shipping, which ships to assign to specific trips according to a given order. Ship routing and scheduling is especially important for industrial and tramp shipping modes, where "routing is the assignment of sequence of harbours to a vessel" and "scheduling is assigning times to the various events on a ships route" (Ronen 1993, p. 326).

The models and decision support systems presented in this thesis span across a wide range of ship routing and scheduling tasks simultaneously. Which of these tasks are accounted for and which not, according to the classification by Christiansen et al. (2007, p. 196) is shown in Table 2.2.

Ships, mainly operating in closed supply chains and in industrial mode, have to prevent an out of stock situation at a delivery harbour and have to assure that production will not stop due to an already full stock at its assigned harbour. This task is part of the inventory ship routing.

Maritime Planning Tasks	Incorporated in this Thesis
Strategic	
Market and trade selection	incorporated (see Chapter 4)
Ship design	incorporated (see Chapter 4)
Network and transportation system design	incorporated (see Chapter 4)
Fleet size and mix decisions	incorporated (see Chapter 4)
Harbour or terminal location, size, and design	incorporated (see Chapter 4)
Tactical	
Fleet size and mix	incorporated (see Chapter 4)
Fleet deployment	incorporated (see Chapter 4)
Ship routing and scheduling	incorporated (see Chapter 4)
Inventory ship routing	not regarded
Berth scheduling	not regarded
Crane scheduling	not regarded
Container yard management	not regarded
Container stowage planning	not regarded
Ship management	not regarded
Distribution of empty containers	not regarded
Operational	
Cruising speed selection	incorporated (see Capter 3)
Ship loading	not regarded
Environmental routing	incorporated (see Capter 3)

Table 2.2: Strategic, tactical and operational planning tasks in maritime transportation according to Christiansen et al. (2007, p. 196)

Operational planning tasks concern the cruising speed, ship loading and environmental routing. When planning the cruising speed, the question is, which average speed has to be selected for the whole voyage between two harbours or which speed to select on single steps of the voyage. This might include travelling at a higher speed at the beginning of a voyage in order to circumnavigate poor weather conditions or vice versa and any combination of speed selections along the route. Usually a predefined latest time of arrival at the destination harbour is given and the objective is to either find a shortest time path or a minimum cost path. Environmental routing incorporates external influences on the ship's behaviour like wind, waves and ocean currents. This planning task is part of the operational routing problem presented in Chapter 3 of this thesis.

In terms of speed, ship owners started to operate their ships in so called slow steaming mode over the last years. This way significant savings in fuel costs can be achieved, since a reduction in speed by 20% reduces the fuel consumption by 50% per time unit (see Christiansen et al. 2007, p. 267). The understanding of the terms full speed steaming, slow steaming and super slow steaming might vary in the maritime transportation environment. In our case full speed steaming represents speeds of 23 ± 1 knots, slow steaming is 18 ± 1 knots and super slow steaming corresponds to 14 ± 1 knots. In practice, ships travel with a higher speed in the direction where the flow of goods is higher. In the opposite direction, ships usually travel slower.

2.3 Routing and Scheduling

A large amount of models that describe land-based vehicle routing and scheduling problems can be found in the corresponding literature. Before presenting models that account for the special characteristics of ships in Section 2.4 the reader is introduced to more general routing and scheduling problems. Some of the models presented might as well be used for modelling ship routing and scheduling problems, which is shown in the following. The easiest way of routing land-based vehicles like trucks is modelling the problem as a standard Vehicle Routing Problem (VRP) or any of its variants. A typical example for making use of an extended vehicle routing model formulation is to describe a parcel service. Usually parcels are distributed to a recipient from a central depot. In order to minimize costs, a parcel service will try to arrange the delivery to its recipients in such a way that the total distance travelled is minimized. With a given road or rail network, the task is to find a minimum distance trip that includes a visit to all potential costumers starting and ending at a given depot. In addition, such a service might also include the pick-up of cargo. This type of problem is called a pick-up and delivery problem, which is an extension of the classical VRP. Here cargo can be dropped off, picked up or both at each visiting point. For the example of a parcel service, customers of consumer goods may have the right to return for instance clothes that do not fit or electronic devices that have a failure within their warranty period. For these cases, companies might allow their customers to have their goods picked up by a parcel service and have them returned to the sender.

In the following a similar problem is described in detail, which has been presented by Karlaftis et al. (2009) as a ship routing problem. They designed a mixed integer programming model for their pick-up and delivery problem of containers. These containers have to be shipped between a central depot (a hub harbour) and many smaller harbours on islands in the Aegean Sea.

Sets and Indices

$k, v \in K$	Set of ship types
$i, j, h \in N$	Set of harbours
0	Depot, mainland harbour

Data

d_i	Demand at harbour i
c_{ijk}	Cost for traversing an arc from harbour i to j
q_k	Capacity of a ship of type k
t_{ijk}	Time for traversing an arc from harbour i to j by a ship of type k
s_{ik}	Necessary time to service harbour i by a ship of type k
tt_k^{max}	Maximum total travel time for a ship of type k
lta_j	Latest arrival time at harbour j
p_j	Pick-up load to be picked up in harbour j
m	Sufficiently large number

Variables

X_{ijk}	1, if a ship of type k is traversing an arc from harbour i to j; 0, otherwise
A_i	Arrival time at harbour i
L_{jk}	Cargo on board of a ship of type k after leaving harbour j

$$min: \sum_i \sum_j \sum_k c_{ijk} \cdot X_{ijk} \tag{2.1}$$

$$\sum_i \sum_k X_{ijk} = 1 \qquad \forall j \tag{2.2}$$

$$\sum_j \sum_k X_{ijk} = 1 \qquad \forall i \tag{2.3}$$

$$\sum_i X_{ihk} = \sum_j X_{hjk} \qquad \forall h, k \tag{2.4}$$

$$\sum_{j \neq 0} X_{0jk} \leq 1 \qquad \forall k \tag{2.5}$$

$$\sum_{i \neq 0} X_{i0k} \leq 1 \qquad \forall k \tag{2.6}$$

$$\sum_i \sum_j X_{ijk} \leq |Q| - 1 \qquad \forall k, Q \subseteq N/0, Q \geq 2 \tag{2.7}$$

Without the index k, the objective function (2.1) and constraints (2.2) to (2.3) plus constraints (2.7) represent a standard Travelling Salesman Problem (TSP). A recent review on the TSP has been provided by Laporte (2010). The objective function is to minimize the costs that arise when travelling on an arc connecting nodes i and j. Nodes for the TSP can be any customer that the salesman has to visit on his round trip. Every customer has to be visited once. In our case the customers are harbours a ship has to visit for loading or unloading activities. Costs for the TSP are often just the travelled distance. For a ship these costs might be the speed dependent fuel costs. Constraints (2.2) and (2.3) imply that every node or in our case harbour has to be visited and left again exactly once. The subtour elimination constraints in (2.7) are the ones presented by Dantzig et al. (1954). Better performing subtour elimination constraints have been developed by Miller et al. (1960) and Gavish (1978). For a comparison of these and newer developed subtour elimination constraints see Langevin et al. (1990). They compare subtour elimination constraints regarding their computational complexity. Subtour elimination constraints avoid multiple smaller round trips for a single vehicle, that are not connected among themselves as shown on the right side of Figure 2.2.

If we regard a node 0 as the home of the salesman, from where he wants to start his voyage and to where he wants to return again, we add constraints

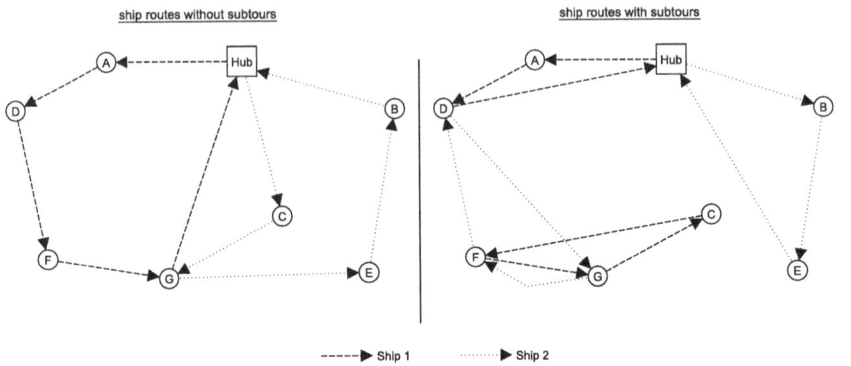

Figure 2.2: Ship routes without and with subtours

(2.5) and (2.6). These constraints force the salesman to start and to end at his origin 0. In case of vehicles this origin and final destination node is often called the depot of a vehicle. For our multiple vehicle case, we also have to assure that no vehicle has subtours and therefore constraints (2.7) have to be constructed for every vehicle or a ship of type k. With the following capacity constraints (2.8) we have a complete Vehicle Routing Problem VRP:

$$\sum_i d_i \left(\sum_j X_{ijk} \right) \leq q_k \qquad \forall k \qquad (2.8)$$

Here a demand d_i is picked up at harbour i if this harbour is visited, which is indicated by variable X_{ijk} and can only be transported, if the capacity q of a ship of type k is not exceeded by this additional demand. VRPs can be enriched by accounting for a permitted total travel time of vehicles as given in constraints (2.9) where the harbour and ship type specific necessary time for service (loading and unloading operations) s_{ik} is added to the arc and ship type dependent travel time t_{ijk}. The sum of service and travel times has to be smaller than a permitted total travel time for a ship of type k given by tt_k^{max}. A description of the development of the vehicle routing problem since its invention in 1959 by Dantzig and Ramser (1959) has again been provided by Laporte (2009).

$$\sum_i s_{ik} \sum_j X_{ijk} + \sum_i \sum_j t_{ijk} \cdot X_{ijk} \leq tt_k^{max} \qquad \forall k \qquad (2.9)$$

If a cargo either has to be picked up and dropped off at a given time or if harbours have specific opening times, Time Windows (TW) are used to describe these constraints (see constraints 2.10 to 2.13).

$$A_j \geq A_i + s_{ik} + t_{ijk} - (1 - X_{ijk}) \cdot tt_k^{max} \qquad \forall i, j, k \qquad (2.10)$$
$$A_j \geq A_i + s_{ik} + t_{ijk} + (1 - X_{ijk}) \cdot tt_k^{max} \qquad \forall i, j, k \qquad (2.11)$$
$$A_0 = 0 \qquad (2.12)$$
$$A_i \leq lta_i \qquad \forall i \qquad (2.13)$$

If a ship of type k does not visit a harbour, decision variable X_{ijk} is 0 and therefore variables A_i and A_j are set to 0 or tt_k^{max} respectively. If the harbours are visited, variables A_i and A_j indicate the arrival times of successive harbours i and j (see Constraints 2.10 and 2.11). Constraint (2.12) sets the departure time for the depot harbour to 0. Constraints (2.13) guarantee that the latest allowed harbour arrival time lta_i is not exceeded.

So far demand could only be picked up at a node or harbour. To be able to also deliver cargo to those nodes, additional pick up and delivery constraints have to be formulated (constraints 2.14 to 2.18).

$$L_{0k} = \sum_i \sum_j d_i \cdot X_{ijk} \qquad \forall k \qquad (2.14)$$
$$L_{jk} \geq L_{0k} - d_j + p_j - m \cdot (1 - X_{0jk}) \qquad \forall j, k \qquad (2.15)$$
$$L_{jk} \geq L_{ik} - d_j + p_j - m \cdot \left(1 - \sum_v X_{ijv}\right) \qquad \forall i, j, k | i \neq j \qquad (2.16)$$
$$L_{0k} \leq q_k \qquad \forall k \qquad (2.17)$$
$$L_{jk} \leq q_k \qquad \forall j, k \qquad (2.18)$$

Constraints (2.14) sum up the cargo on board a ship of type k when reaching its depot or mainland harbour. The cargo on board is allocated to harbours, that are visited after leaving the mainland harbour (depot) and have been picked up at some other island harbours. This is cargo that stays on board a ship when entering the mainland harbour. Constraints (2.15) and (2.16) sum up the cargo, that is unloaded and loaded on board at the mainland harbour or any island harbour respectively. Furthermore capacity constraints (2.17) and (2.18) guarantee that a ship's capacity is not exceeded.

As mentioned above, this pick-up and delivery problem can be transferred from this maritime application to any road based application where only the mode of transportation changes from ships to for example trucks, as far as wheel times are not exceeded.

As an example of a vehicle routing or pick-up and delivery problem with a similar problem to solve for trucks and ships can be found in Nishimura et al. (2009), Aas et al. (2007) or Gribkovskaia et al. (2008). All these decision problems are ship routing problems for feeder services. As mentioned earlier, feeder services operate within a local, mainly short sea environment, delivering cargo (mainly containers) from a hub harbour to spoke harbours and simultaneously picking up cargo at those spoke harbours with the hub harbour or any spoke harbour as destination on the ship's round trip.

Another often found way of operating trains, trucks and aircraft can be transferred to tramp shipping. Here, the typical task is to find an optimal route for delivering a full vehicle load from its pick-up location to its destination. If the capacity is not fully utilized, shippers try to find optional spot cargo that has to be delivered from the same pick-up to the same destination location as the mandatory cargo. After having dropped off this cargo, the shipper is then interested in finding a new order, that has the same pick-up location as the last delivery location or at least a location close to that (as an example see Figure 2.3).

The example in Figure 2.3 shows a possible path of two different ships transporting seven different cargoes between their origin and destination harbour. The cargoes are labeled by their origin and destination harbour. Ship 1's harbour call sequence is A, B, I, D, K, B, E directly starting out with an empty leg from harbours A to B (e.g. without carrying any cargo). Another empty leg is between harbours K and B. Ship 2's harbour calling sequence is F, J, K, E, A, C again with two empty legs between harbours J, K and E, A. This kind of problem can be modelled as a Pick-up and Delivery Problem (PDP) as described by Norstad et al. (2011) and presented in detail in the following for a tramp shipping problem:

Sets and Indices

$i, j \in H$	Set of harbours at which cargoes can be loaded
$i + n \in H$	Corresponding unloading harbour for cargo picked up in harbour i
H_p	Set of pick-up harbours
H_d	Set of delivery harbours
$H_c \subset H_p$	Set of pick-up harbours for mandatory cargo
$H_o \subset H_p$	Set of pick-up harbours for optional cargo
$k \in K$	Set of ship types
$H_k \subset (H_p \cup H_d)$	Cargo at set of Harbours, corresponding to cargo a ship of type k can load

$H_{pk}; H_{dk}$	Set of all pick-up and delivery harbours for cargo a ship of type k can load
$o_k; d_k$	Origin and destination of a ship of type k, either harbour or artificial position at sea

Data

cap_k	Capacity of a ship of type k
qc_i	Weight of cargo from harbour i
$\overline{tw_i}, \underline{tw_i}$	Time interval for each harbour and cargo combination i
s_{ik}	Necessary time to service harbour i by a ship of type k
t_{ijk}	Time for traversing an arc from harbour i to j by a ship of type k
rev_i^h	Revenue for loading cargo from harbour i
c_{ijk}	Cost for traversing an arc from harbour i to j for a ship of type k

Variables

X_{ijk}	1, if a ship of type k is traversing an arc from harbour i to j; 0, otherwise
A_{ik}	Arrival time at harbour i of a ship of type k
L_{jk}	Cargo on board of a ship of type k after leaving harbour j

$$max : \sum_{k} \sum_{i \in H_k} \sum_{j \in H_k} rev_i^h \cdot X_{ijk} - \sum_{k} \sum_{i \in H_k} \sum_{j \in H_k} c_{ijk} \cdot X_{ijk} \tag{2.19}$$

The objective function (2.19) maximizes the profit obtained by subtracting all travel dependent costs from the revenue received from transporting cargoes from harbours i to their destination harbour $i + n$.

$$\sum_{k} \sum_{j \in H_k} X_{ijk} = 1 \qquad \forall i \in H_c \tag{2.20}$$

$$\sum_{k} \sum_{j \in H_k} X_{ijk} \leq 1 \qquad \forall i \in H_o \tag{2.21}$$

$$\sum_{j \in H_{pk} \bigcup d_k} X_{o_k jk} = 1 \qquad \forall k \tag{2.22}$$

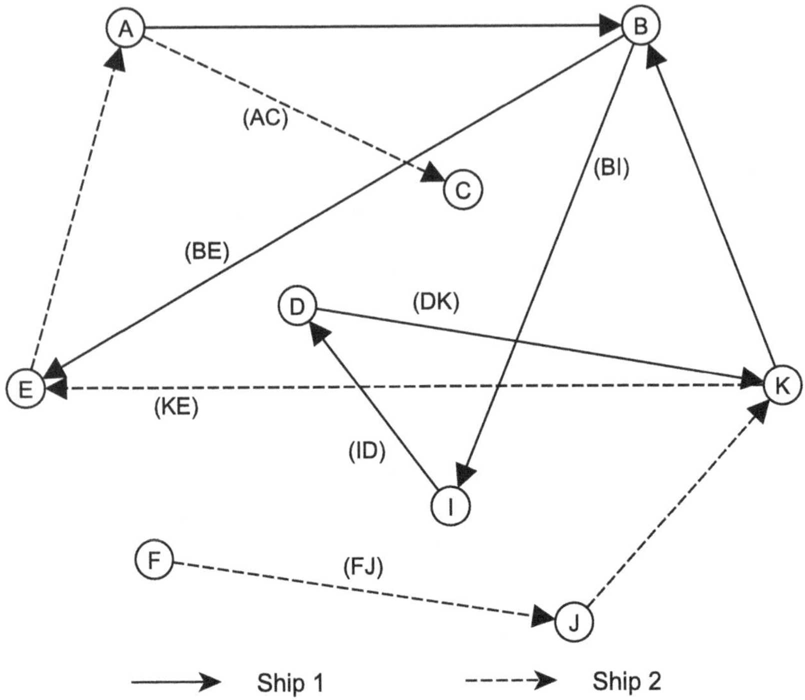

Figure 2.3: Tramp ship routing example, on the basis of Lin and Liu (2011, p. 415)

$$\sum_{i \in H_k} X_{ijk} - \sum_{i \in H_k} X_{jik} = 0 \qquad \forall k, j \in H_k \ \{o_k, d_k\} \tag{2.23}$$

$$\sum_{i \in H_{dk} \bigcup o_k} X_{id_k k} = 1 \qquad \forall k \tag{2.24}$$

$$\sum_{j \in H_k} X_{ijk} - \sum_{j \in H_k} X_{j,i+n,k} = 0 \qquad \forall k, i \in H_{pk} \tag{2.25}$$

$$A_{ik} + s_{ik} + t_{i,i+n,k} - A_{i+n,k} \leq 0 \qquad \forall k, i \in H_{pk} \tag{2.26}$$

$$X_{ijk} \left(A_{ik} + s_{ik} + t_{ijk} - A_{jk} \right) \leq 0 \qquad \forall k, i, j \tag{2.27}$$

$$\underline{tw_i} \leq t_{ik} \leq \overline{tw_i} \qquad \forall k, i \in H_k \tag{2.28}$$

$$X_{ijk} \left(L_{ik} + qc_j - L_{jk} \right) = 0 \qquad \forall k, j \in H_{pk}, (i,j) \in H_k \tag{2.29}$$

$$X_{i,j+n,k} \left(L_{ik} - qc_j - L_{j+n,k} \right) = 0 \qquad \forall k, j \in H_{pk}, (i, j+n) \in H_k \tag{2.30}$$

$$L_{o_k k} = 0 \qquad \forall k \quad (2.31)$$

$$\sum_j qc_i X_{ijk} \leq L_{ik} \leq \sum_j cap_k X_{ijk} \qquad \forall k, i \in H_{pk} \quad (2.32)$$

$$0 \leq L_{i+n,k} \leq \sum_j (cap_k - qc_i) X_{i+n,j,k} \qquad \forall k, i \in H_{pk} \quad (2.33)$$

$$X_{ijk} \in \{0, 1\} \qquad \forall k, i, j \quad (2.34)$$

Network flow constraints (2.20) to (2.25) are very similar to constraints (2.2) to (2.6) already introduced for the VRP of Karlaftis et al. (2009). Constraints (2.20) guarantee that all mandatory cargo has to be transported and therefore the pick-up harbour has to be visited, whereas constraints (2.21) state that optional spot cargo can also be picked up, but does not have to be transported. The network flow constraints are given in (2.22) to (2.24). Constraints (2.25) ensure that, if a cargo has been picked up in its pick-up harbour, it has to be dropped off at the cargo's corresponding destination harbour. A delivery harbour of a cargo should only be visited if its pick-up harbour has been visited beforehand. This is ensured by constraints (2.26). Constraints (2.27) sum up all travelling and service times of the last harbour visited, to calculate the arrival time at the next harbour. These non-linear formulated constraints can be linearised the same way as done in (2.10) and (2.11) which represent similar constraints. The remaining constraints are loading and time window constraints (2.28) within which a cargo has to be picked up and dropped off. These loading constraints guarantee that cargo is added onto the already present cargo for pick up operations (2.29) and subtracted for unloading operations (2.30). Constraints (2.31) ensure that no cargo is on board a ship of type k at its initial position. The remaining two constraints prior to the binary restrictions of the flow variable (2.34) are capacity constraints ensuring that the total amount of cargo loaded does not exceed the capacity of ships of type k (2.32 and 2.33).

Since trucks, aircraft and trains usually are not able to change their travel speed above a given limit due to physical (aircraft and trains) or governmental restrictions (speed regulations for trucks) or volume of traffic in the same network (trains) the speed as a variable has been removed from the above model. But ships can, except for coastal or harbour regions, change speed in the open sea. This is the reason why Norstad et al. (2011) consider a variable speed setting within a given feasible range, indicated by following additional constraints:

$$\underline{v_k} \leq V_{ijk} \leq \overline{v_k} \qquad \forall k, i, j \qquad (2.35)$$

Here decision variable $V_{ij,k}$ is the speed a ship of type k should travel at when traversing on an arc from a harbour i to a harbour j. This speed is not allowed to be lower than $\underline{v_k}$ and higher than $\overline{v_k}$, the given minimum and maximum speed ships of type k can travel at. Additionally, the costs in the objective function (2.19) are replaced by speed dependent cost $(c_k(V_{ijk}))$ and are multiplied by the distance (d_{ij}) between two consecutive harbours i and j $(c_k(V_{ijk}) \cdot d_{ij})$. The multiplication of this term with decision variable X_{ijk} turns objective function (2.19) into a non-linear function. Then t_{ijk}, the time for traversing from harbour i to harbour j with a ship of type k, is replaced by d_{ij}/V_{ijk}, the speed dependent travel time in constraints (2.26) and (2.27).

Characteristic for these types of transportation problems is that the vehicle does not return to a local depot, which can often be found in air, tramp ship and rail road transportation. Often, it is also required for these three transportation modes that cargo is directly transported from its pick-up to its destination harbour without additional stops at nodes or train stations, airports or harbours.

Another way of operation that can occur for land-based, air and water-based transportation is a ferry service. The task for planning a ferry service can be considered as a service network design problem (SDNP). Compared to all other routing and scheduling models introduced so far following example refers to passenger transportation and not to general cargo transportation. This model, formulated as a multicommodity network flow problem, might also be used for general cargo transportation by replacing passengers with general cargo with given demand for each harbour to harbour (or node to node) relation. These node or harbour relations called origin-destination (OD) pairs represent the amount of passengers (cargo) to be transported from an origin node to a destination node with a given point in time a specific demand arrives for service at its origin node. The SDNP has originally been used in the same or similar way as described in the following for other modes of transportation. Yan and Tseng (2002) and Barnhart et al. (2002) adopted the SDNP for an airline routing and scheduling problem where a network is designed in such a way that passenger demands for travelling from one airport to the other is best satisfied by a given aircraft fleet. Another passenger transportation application can be found in Yan and Chen (2002) where the task is to find an inter-city bus network design and timetable setting for buses operating in Taiwan. Two examples with the use of similar model formulations for transporting general cargo are given in Farvolden and Powell (1994) for truck routing and Barnhart and Schneur (1996) for express shipments by air.

The following model has been presented by Lai and Lo (2004). An extension of the same model designing a service network for multiple ferry services operating in and around Hong Kong has been described by Wang and Lo (2008).

Sets and Indices

$d \in R$	Set of origin and destination pairs
N, A	Set of nodes and arcs for the ferry network
$N^b, N^e \subset N$	Set of nodes at the beginning and ending of the planning interval
N_d, A_d	Set of nodes and arcs for the passenger network
S, S_d	Set of service arcs for the ferry and passenger network
W, W_d	Set of waiting arcs for the ferry and passenger network
O_d	Origin arcs of the passenger network
D_d	Destination arcs of the passenger network

Data

cf	Fixed costs for hiring or owning a ferry per day
c_{ij}	Costs for operating a trip between harbours i and j
f	Maximum number of ferries
d_{di}	Passenger demand of origin-destination pair d for harbours $i \in N_d$
cap	Ferry capacity
t_{ij}	Travel time between harbour i and j
tt_d	Travel time of origin destination pair d for direct service
β	Progressing time between two consecutive service arcs
rev_d^c	Revenue for origin destination pair d
wv	Waiting time value
tv	Travel time value
$\overline{u_{ij}}$	Upper bound on ferry flow on arc connecting harbours i and j
$\overline{u_{dij}}$	Upper bound on passenger flow on an arc connecting harbours i and j

Variables

X_{dij}	Passenger flow in a time-space network of origin destination pair d
Y_{ij}	Ferry flow in the ferry time-space network

The set of all arcs A consists of all service arcs S, waiting arcs W, and nodes N. The underlying network is shown in Figure 2.4. Within this ferry network a ferry can either travel on a service arc to the next node or is waiting at the same node (pier) between two time periods. Similar to that the passenger time-space networks $G(N_d, A_d)$ consists of nodes N_d and arcs A_d for each OD pair d. Where A_d again is the joined set of all wait arcs W_d and service arcs S_d.

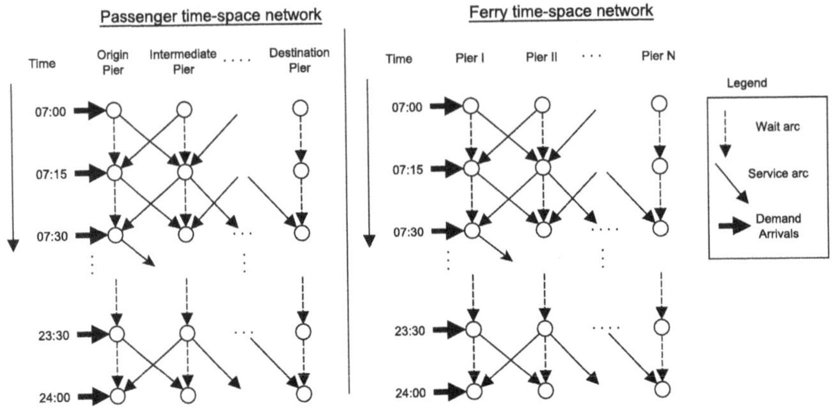

Figure 2.4: Passenger and ferry time-space network, according to Lai and Lo (2004, p. 309, 310)

The objective function (2.36) minimizes the sum of all operating and penalty costs where the first term sums up all fixed costs for owning or hiring a ferry for this planning interval. The second term represents all travel costs for travelling from a node i to a node j. Terms three and four represent all penalty costs which consist of passenger waiting costs and costs for multi-stop trips. A multi-stop trip is less favourable for passengers as the total travel time is increasing with each intermediate stop. Last, all revenue received from offering this transportation service is subtracted.

$$
\begin{aligned}
min : \sum_{i \in N^b} \sum_{j \in N \setminus N^b} Y_{ij} \cdot cf + \sum_{i,j \in S} Y_{ij} \cdot c_{ij} + \\
\sum_{d} \sum_{i,j \in (W_d, O_d)} X_{dij} \cdot wv \cdot \beta + \\
\sum_{d} \left(\sum_{i,j \in S_d} X_{dij} \cdot t_{ij} - X_{dij \in D_d} \cdot tt_d \right) \cdot tv -
\end{aligned}
$$

$$\sum_{d} \sum_{i,j \in D_d} X_{dij} \cdot rev_d^c \tag{2.36}$$

$$\sum_{j \in N} Y_{ij} - \sum_{k \in N} Y_{ki} = 0 \qquad \forall i \in N \backslash \left(N^b \bigcup N^e \right) \tag{2.37}$$

$$\sum_{i \in N^b} \sum_{j \in N \backslash N^b} Y_{ij} \leq f \tag{2.38}$$

$$\sum_{j \in N_d} X_{dij} - \sum_{k \in N_d} X_{dki} = d_{di} \qquad \forall i \in N_d, d \tag{2.39}$$

$$\sum_{d} X_{dij} \leq Y_{ij} \cdot cap \qquad \forall i, j \in S \tag{2.40}$$

$$0 \leq X_{dij} \leq \overline{u_{dij}} \qquad \forall i, j \in A_d, O_d, D_d, d \tag{2.41}$$

$$0 \leq Y_{ij} \leq \overline{u_{ij}} \qquad \forall i, j \in A \tag{2.42}$$

Constraints (2.37) denote the ferry flow conservation constraints stating that every node being visited has to be left again. Constraints (2.38) limit the number of ferries used. Constraints (2.39) are the passenger flow conservation constraints that also indicate at which nodes passengers are entering or leaving the ferry. Capacity constraints (2.40) sum up all passenger flows and guarantees that these do not exceed the ferry's capacity. Last, constraints (2.41) and (2.42) formulate upper and lower bounds for all passenger and ferry flows between nodes i and j respectively.

A SDNP only takes a small time section as a planning interval and tries to match a passenger demand with a given fleet of vehicles. Compared to the later introduced strategic liner shipping service network design problem vehicles do not necessarily return to their original positions and therefore do not perform round trips as needed for the liner shipping service network. But as stated earlier this model formulation very well suits the planning tasks of other modes of transportation.

Literature on truck, train and aircraft routing and scheduling can be found in Cordeau et al. (1998) for rail transportation, Crainic (2003) for long-haul transportation, Crainic and Kim (2007) for intermodal transportation and Crainic (2000) for the above introduces service network design in freight transportation.

2.4 Routing and Scheduling in Maritime Shipping

Extensive literature reviews on ship routing and scheduling are given in Kjeldsen (2009), Christiansen et al. (2004, 2007) and Ronen (1983, 1993). In contrast to truck vehicle routing problems, little work has been done on ship routing and scheduling. Increasing fuel costs and consumer expectations to reduce carbon dioxide and sulphur emission during the transport of products are forcing ship owners and shipping companies not only to minimize costs but also to minimize ship's emissions. In addition, governments are planning to enact the use of even more expensive diesel instead of heavy fuel oil for ocean going ships on their territorial waters. To comply with this framework, vessels are already operated in slow steaming mode for for the purpose of cost and emission reduction purposes. A reduction in speed has significant impact, since vessel fuel consumption has a cubic function in regard to speed.

To show the effect of slow steaming a model for determining emissions as presented by Kranke (2009) can be used. In this model the specific energy consumption at reduced speed (EC_{red}) measured in gram fuel consumed per transported ton and kilometre, is obtained as follows:

$$EC_{red} = EC_{nor} \left(\frac{V_{red}}{V_{nor}} \right)^2 \left[\frac{g}{tkm} \right] \tag{2.43}$$

The energy consumption EC_{nor} for the normal speed is multiplied by the squared fraction of reduced speed V_{red} to the normal speed setting V_{nor}. The CO_2 emission measured in grams CO_2 per transported ton and kilometre results from multiplying the energy consumption with the CO_2-factor (for different CO_2-factors, according to different ship size, see Kranke 2009, p. 38).

$$CO_2\text{-}Emission = EC \cdot (CO_2\text{-}factor) \left[\frac{g_{CO_2}}{tkm} \right] \tag{2.44}$$

As a numerical example a TEU loaded with 14 tons of goods has to be shipped from Hamburg to New York. We will compare the CO_2 emission when travelling at a normal speed of 23 knots with a reduced speed of 18 knots on a 8,000 TEU ship. With an energy consumption of 4.84 [g/tkm] of this ship type at normal speed, the reduced energy consumption results in:

$$EC_{red} = 4.84 \left[\frac{g_{HFO}}{tkm} \right] \cdot \left(\frac{18kn}{23kn} \right)^2 = 2.96 \left[\frac{g}{tkm} \right] \tag{2.45}$$

For a distance of 6,526 kilometres (3,524 nm) between Hamburg and New York the amount of CO_2 emitted in kg at a speed of 23 knots and a CO_2-factor of 3.114 grams CO_2 per gram heavy fuel oil (HFO) sums up to:

$$CO_2\text{-}Emission_{23kn} = 4.84\left[\frac{g_{HFO}}{tkm}\right]\cdot 3.114\left[\frac{g_{CO_2}}{g_{HFO}}\right] = 15.07\left[\frac{g_{CO_2}}{tkm}\right] \quad (2.46)$$

$$\Rightarrow 15.07\left[\frac{g_{CO_2}}{tkm}\right]\cdot 14\,[t]\cdot 6,526\,[km] = 1,376.9\,[kg] \quad (2.47)$$

and at 18 knots:

$$CO_2\text{-}Emission_{18kn} = 2.96\left[\frac{g_{HFO}}{tkm}\right]\cdot 3.114\left[\frac{g_{CO_2}}{g_{HFO}}\right] = 9.22\left[\frac{g_{CO_2}}{tkm}\right] \quad (2.48)$$

$$\Rightarrow 9.22\left[\frac{g_{CO_2}}{tkm}\right]\cdot 14\,[t]\cdot 6,526\,[km] = 842.4\,[kg] \quad (2.49)$$

The speed reduction of 28% results in a CO_2 reduction of 63%.

Most likely ship owners will only operate their fleets in slow steam mode, as long as its profitability increases. A paper presented by Cariou (2011) states that emissions have been reduced by 11% from 2009 to 2010 and that the bunker break-even price of at least 259$ per ton IFO will not lead to a situation where carriers return to normal speed in the near future. The break-even price indicates the price of bunker fuel, from which on slow steaming is beneficial for a ship, operating at a given cargo rate and demand. With a current bunker fuel price of over 600$ for IFO380 at Rotterdam harbour (Bunkerworld 2011) and steadily increasing, even more ship operators will restrain from returning to normal speed. Note, for specific trade routes on which the berthing times are high in regard to voyage times (e.g. Australia / Oceania and Latin America / Caribbean) the break-even-point is 568$ and 556$ respectively and in this case slow steaming might not lead to profit maximization if bunker prices slightly fall.

To meet their schedules, a lot of effort has been put into reducing ship's demurrage time in harbours. The increase of the maximum permitted harbour to harbour travel time allows cruising with reduced speed. An articles concerning the reduction of demurrage can be found in (Christiansen et al. 2004, p. 12). The approach concentrated on in this thesis uses alternative vessel propulsion modes to reduce costs and emissions of a whole fleet in a supply network. In the following a selection of the most recent research about the field of ship routing and scheduling will be presented. Note, the focus will lie on the water side planning tasks.

2.4.1 Examples of Operational and Tactical Planning

Operational Planning

Considerable research has been done on ship routing and scheduling under an operational perspective by optimizing the efficiency of harbour to harbour routing. In short sea shipping the aim is to minimize the travel distance and estimate the time of arrival by circumnavigating coastlines or shallow waters (Fagerholt et al. 2000). Further literature close to our operational, environmental shortest path problem are given in Section 3.1 (see Page 40).

Another operational planning task is to prevent a ship from stability problems, by planning the container stowage accordingly. Examples of container stowage planning tasks can be found in Wilson and Roach (2000) and Kang and Kim (2002).

In cases of overbooking or a no-show of accepted cargo, shipping companies have to decide which containers to load and if capacity is exceeded, which cargo to book on later ships. This problem is addressed in Ang et al. (2007). Their multi-period sea cargo mix problem is solved with heuristic algorithms providing fast and nearly optimal solutions for this time critical operational planning problem. Based on surcharges, higher or lower prices and costs, the most profitable cargo is transported and others rejected.

Tactical Planning

An example of a tactical planning problem in maritime transportation with the objective of minimizing fuel emissions by optimizing speed on shipping routes, is given by Fagerholt et al. (2010). This problem can be used in a tramp- or industrial shipping setting, where a certain amount of cargo orders is known at specific harbours for the near future and have to be planned in such a way that fuel emissions are reduced by optimizing the speed on each harbour-to-harbour relation and simultaneously satisfying the harbours time windows. In this case the time windows might depend on the earliest pick-up time of a cargo at its loading harbour and its latest arrival time at its unloading harbour. Environmental influences such as wind, waves and currents are not accounted for. Significant savings of fuel (24.3%) and emissions (19.4%) can be achieved by the described shortest path approaches with different optimized average speed settings on each harbour-to-harbour realtion, instead of travelling with the same constant speed on all harbour relations.

An inventory routing problem, also classified as a tactical planning problem, is presented by Grønhaug et al. (2010) who solve the problem by use of a branch-and-price method. Branch-and-price methods use a branch-and-bound algorithm, where upper bounds are calculated by a column generation technique. This inventory routing problem, that we will present in detail, has been designed for a company transporting liquefied natural gas (LNG). In this industrial shipping context, the task is to prevent an out-of-stock situation at consumption harbours, where the LNG is regasified to natural gas (NG). Additionally, the LNG storage capacity at harbours where the NG is cooled down in the liquefaction plants, shall also not be exceeded. LNG tankers now have to be scheduled in a way that all constraints are fulfilled. In their mathematical model formulation binary variables Λ_{kr} represent the columns of the column generation approach, which have value 1 if a ship of type k is travelling on route r, or 0 otherwise. The design of routes is part of the branch-and-price's subproblem which will not be presented here in detail.

Sets and Indices

N^P	Set of pick-up harbours, liquefaction plants
N^D	Set of delivery harbours, regasification terminals
$k \in K$	Set of ship types
$i, j \in N = N^P \cup N^D$	Set of harbours
$r \in R_k$	Set of routes for ships of type k
$t \in T$	Set of time periods

Data

s_{it}^{LNG}	Lower bound on sales of LNG in harbour i and time period t
p_{it}	Upper bound on production of LNG in harbour i and time period t
rev_{it}^{g}	Revenue obtained from transporting and selling gas in harbour i and time period t
cp_{it}	Costs for producing LNG in harbour i and time period t
$\overline{inv_i}$	Upper bound on inventory level of LNG in harbour i
$\underline{inv_i}$	Lower bound on inventory level of LNG in harbour i
h_i	Harbour visiting indicator has value +1 for delivery harbours and -1 for pick-up harbours i
x_{ijktr}	1, if a ship of type k (un-)loads at harbour i in t before travelling to harbour j on route r; 0, otherwise
z_{iktr}	1, if ship k visits harbour i in t on route r; 0, otherwise
q_{iktr}	(Un-)Loading volume at harbour i by a ship of type k in time period t on route r
l_{iktr}	Number of tanks unloaded from ship of type k at harbour i in t on route r
w_k	Number of tanks on ship k
ct_{kr}	Costs for a ship of type k travelling on route r
$ncap_i$	Number of ships that can unload simultaneously in harbour i
$tcap_k$	Maximum number of tanks in ship of type k

Variables

Y_{it}	Sales or production of LNG in harbour i in time period t
S_{it}	Inventory level of storage in harbour i in time period t
Λ_{kr}	Number of round trips a ship of type k makes on its assigned route r during one planning interval

$$max: \sum_{i \in N^D} \sum_t rev_{it}^g \cdot Y_{it} - \sum_{i \in N^P} \sum_t cp_{it} \cdot Y_{it} - \sum_k \sum_r ct_{kr} \Lambda_{kr} \qquad (2.50)$$

The objective function (2.50) maximizes the profit obtained from revenues subtracted by production and transportation costs and is subject to following constraints:

$$S_{it} - S_{i,t-1} - \sum_k \sum_r h_i \cdot q_{iktr} \Lambda_{kr} + h_i \cdot Y_{it} = 0 \qquad \forall i, t \qquad (2.51)$$

$$\sum_k \sum_r z_{iktr} \cdot \Lambda_{kr} \leq ncap_i \qquad \forall i, t \qquad (2.52)$$

$$\underline{inv_i} \leq S_{it} \leq \overline{inv_i} \qquad \forall i, t \qquad (2.53)$$

$$s_{it}^{LNG} \leq Y_{it} \leq p_{it} \qquad \forall i, t \qquad (2.54)$$

$$\sum_r \Lambda_{kr} = 1 \qquad \forall k \qquad (2.55)$$

$$\sum_r l_{iktr} \cdot \Lambda_{kr} \leq tcap_k \qquad \forall i \in N^D, k, t \qquad (2.56)$$

$$\sum_r x_{ijktr} \cdot \Lambda_{kr} \leq 1 \qquad \forall i, j, k, t \qquad (2.57)$$

Constraints (2.51) guarantee that inventory capacity in the pick-up and delivery harbours is neither exceeded nor that an out of stock situation occurs. The berth capacity constraints (2.52) prevent that an upper bound of maximum allowed ships in the harbour for unloading or loading activities is surpassed. The amount of LNG stored (see constraints 2.53) and the amount of LNG produced (see constraints 2.54) has to stay within a given interval. Convexity constraints (2.55) assure that each ship type is assigned to only one route. For each ship type k the number of cargo tanks unloaded in delivery harbours i must be smaller than the maximum number of tanks on the ship (see constraints 2.56). Constraints (2.57) indicate in which time period t a ship of type k is visiting harbour j after having visited harbour i on route r.

Another inventory routing problem with the aim of transferring liquid bulk products from production harbours to consumption harbours is presented in Al-Khayyal and Hwang (2007). The mixed integer model approach minimizes all costs for ships with different compartments, capable of transporting different product types. A very similar mixed integer programming approach, which additionally takes into consideration the blending of grain products is shown in Bilgen and Ozkarahan (2007).

Two examples for the tramp shipping industry transporting bulk cargo are the ones described by Brønmo et al. (2007) and Korsvik et al. (2010). Both consider additional optional spot cargo that can be transported on top of a mandatory given order. The mandatory bulk cargo has to be transported due to long-term contracts, whereas spot cargo will only be transported if this is profitable under given ship's capacity and harbour entering constraints. To solve models, Brønmo et al. (2007) use a multi-start local search heuristic, whereas Korsvik et al. (2010) are able to show that their tabu search heuristic performs even better than that of Brønmo et al. (2007), which has been tested for 13 real data case instances. The decision on whether or not to transport optional spot cargo is very time sensitive. Therefore heuristics are used to find good feasible solutions and to uphold a short response time.

Korsvik et al. (2011) improved their last mentioned approach by allowing split loads and stochastic demand. Again, mandatory bulk cargo has to be loaded and optional spot cargo can be transported additionally on the remaining unused capacities. They propose a large neighbourhood search heuristic for solving this problem. With this extension they were able to show that a better utilisation a ship's capacity has a significant impact on the revenue generated. With a rise in fuel price the beneficial effect is even larger.

A very similar problem is also described by Lin and Liu (2011). They use a genetic solution approach to simultaneously solve a ship allocation, freight assignment and ship routing problem in a tramp shipping environment. Compared to Korsvik et al. (2011) they do not allow for split loads and also do not account for stochastic demand.

Another tramp ship routing and scheduling problem considering variable speed settings on arcs between two successive harbours is subject to research from Norstad et al. (2011). Within given time windows for loading and unloading specific cargoes, the variable speed arrangement allows for additional spot cargo to be shipped. That way revenue is increased compared to fixed speed settings where this additional spot cargo might not have been transported due to the given time window constraints. Furthermore, even with a typical cubic function of fuel consumption and likewise rising costs with increasing speed, higher costs due to only partly raised speed do not exceed the revenue gain from variable speeds. This model is presented in Section 2.3 (see Page 20) without the speed selection as a typical tramp shipping or truck and aircraft routing problem.

A combined Fleet Size & Mix Problem and Fleet Deployment Problem for a liner shipping network design and cargo booking task has been stated by Meng and Wang (2010). They call their problem a short-term Liner Ship Fleet Planning Problem where the shipment of forecasted cargo demand has to be satisfied by a given liner service schedule. The objective is to minimize the total operating costs by varying the fleet size and mix (amount and type of ships used) at a given harbour visiting frequency. The main task of this model is to consider an uncertain cargo demand distribution while maintaining a promised service level. This problem has been solved as a chance constraint mixed integer programming model.

Another paper on the Fleet Size & Mix Problem by Meng and Wang (2011) states that ships should only be chartered on a short-term basis. For a long-term planning horizon it is cheaper to purchase ships. Their multi-period liner ship fleet planning problem (MPLSFP) under given deterministic container shipment demand has been modelled as a scenario-based dynamic programming approach and can be solved by any shortest path algorithm.

2.4.2 Examples of Strategic Planning

Several articles are covering the problem of optimizing the schedule of a ship fleet within a given supply chain which is according to Christiansen et al. (2007, see Pages 201, 220) a strategic planning task. Appelgren (1969) is the first to describe a problem that solves the optimal sequence of cargoes each ship of a fleet should transport under given time limits.

Ronen (1986) defines the minimal fleet operating costs under storage and handling constraints at the harbours.

A further aspect being considered in a supply chain including maritime transportation can again be the inventory in harbours of the described supply chain. Christiansen (1999) presents a mixed integer programming model for optimizing a pick-up and delivery problem under inventory and time constraints in a supply chain, when ammonia has to be transported by ships between production and consumption harbours. These inventory routing problems can also be modelled with variable vessel speed by set partitioning (e.g. Brown et al. 1987).

Similar to Brown et al., Fisher and Rosenwein (1989) solve the selection problem of alternative operating speed by the use of a different set partitioning approach.

Papadakis and Perakis (1990) even show a method for finding the optimal speed selection in a ship routing pick-up and delivery problem.

Brown et al. (2007) describe a problem, where different operating modes for navy vessels save up to 12.5% of fuel by only varying the engine setting.

In many cases liner shipping network design as a strategic planning problem deals with the question, whether to have a fleet of ships travelling at a lower speed but with the need of more ships or, travelling at a higher speed and therefore using fewer ships. To show the influence of the selected average fleet speed on the fleet size an example calculation is introduced. V is the average speed of the fleet when travelling on a liner service round trip. N_S is the number of ships needed to uphold a promised visiting frequency F (e.g. once a week) at all harbours. N_H is the number of visited harbours and T_H is the average time spent in a harbour for loading and unloading activities. Δ accounts for the total travelled distance of one round trip.

$$N_S \geq \left(N_H \cdot T_H + \frac{\Delta}{V} \right) \cdot F \tag{2.58}$$

For an example following values are assumed: $V = 22$ kn; $F = 1/168$; $N_H = 13$; $T_H = 22h$; $\Delta = 23,276nm$. Using formula (2.58) given by Notteboom and Vernimmen (2009), we receive $N_S = 8$ for a speed of $22kn$. Reducing the speed to $19kn$ leads to $N_S \geq 8.99$. As a result at least one more ship is needed to maintain the same service at a reduced speed.

A similar planning task has been addressed by Ronen (2011). He finds, that when considering fuel costs, it is beneficial to operate ships within a container liner shipping environment at their minimal-cost speed for the resulting amount of ships needed to guarantee a given harbour visiting frequency. The optimal selection of speed combined with the number of vessels needed to perform a permanent route round trip at minimum costs, is addressed in Chapter 4.

The problem of assigning limited container carrying capacity to different carriers within an alliance has been addressed by Agarwal and Ergun (2010). They use an allocation mechanism which combines mathematical programming and game theory in order to find the optimal collaboration strategy. Every carrier who's aim is to maximize his own profits, is encouraged in efficiently participating in this alliance by incentive side payments.

A model that analyses the influence of ship sizes on the total transport cost of a standard container within an intermodal transportation system is shown by Schönknecht (2007). He finds out, that the use of Super-Post-Panamax ships, with a capacity of up to 14,000 TEU, will reduce transportation costs of containers. But with increasing size, ships are limited to only a few harbours that they can call at. Due to their container holding capacity, more containers have to be loaded and unloaded in harbours, which also leads to longer berthing times.

A simulation based optimisation approach in an intermodal freight transportation environment which investigates the fleet size and mix container liner shipping decisions, has been presented by Dong and Song (2012). They analyse the influence of hinterland transportation times and its uncertainty on the optimal fleet size of container liner services.

A service network design and a combined asset management problem solved with a branch-and-price algorithm, has been presented by ?. Their master problem solves the multicommodity network design problem under given vehicle management constraints. The column-generation based problem branches into two additional subproblems. One subproblem generates the vehicle dependent cycles and the other subproblem generates the path-flows for each cargo transported. This model is not only applicable to maritime transportation, but has also been tested on real-life based rail transportation case instances.

The question whether to design multi-harbour or hub & spoke networks for container ship liner services has been studied by Imai et al. (2009). A multi-harbour network is a round trip of a liner service with multiple harbours to be called at, whereas in a hub & spoke network configuration, larger ships operate between major transshipment hubs from where smaller feeder ships service local harbours in a spoke network. Imai et al. (2009) choose a two stage approach with the first step being the service network design and the second step being the container distribution across the liner service. The result of their research is, that even when considering mega-containerships with a capacity of more than 20,000 TEU, multi-harbour networks are more beneficial than hub & spoke networks, when empty container repositioning is a vital part of the underlying problem.

Literature on the strategic planning tasks for liner services will also be partly discussed in Chapter 4.

Chapter 3

Environmental Routing

Ships are affected by a multitude of environmental influences such as: tides, currents, waves and winds. The choice of a shortest route or path in terms of e.g. costs, fuel or time between two consecutive harbours or any coordinates and considering environmental influences for this shortest route, is called environmental routing (see Christiansen et al. 2007, p. 265). Data obtained from our operational, environmental routing approach are an important basis to our strategic liner network design. Without calculating the weather dependent route distance, travel time and most important fuel consumption as average values for each season of the year, the strategic network design would not be affected by environmental influences.

In the following we will present how we calculate the above mentioned data for each possible harbour to harbour relation for all 33 harbours we take into consideration. These harbours are located around the Atlantic Ocean and the Gulf of Mexico to which we will refer to as the set of harbours in the following.

According to Christiansen et al. (2007, p. 196) the so called environmental routing is classified as an operational planning problem. Algorithms that solve environmental routing problems are usually used to calculate a minimum time, distance or fuel consumption a priori for a ship leaving a harbour for its next destination. Weather data used for such Shortest Path Problems (SPP) are forecasted weather conditions. SPPs are problems, where the objective is to find the minimum distance from a starting point to a destination point of a given network. In the following we will refer to points in a network as nodes and all lines connecting these nodes are called arcs. In our case, since we are interested in average weather conditions over all four seasons of the year, we take weather data from reanalysis of the year 2009 (for detailed descriptions see Section 3.5 on weather data).

The outline of this chapter is as follows. Before we describe the underlying network design of the SPP considered here (see Section 3.2), we will shortly present a literature review of other approaches on the environmental routing problem in Section 3.1. In Section 3.3 the SPPs and especially the enhanced label-setting algorithm, that is capable of solving the SPP with Time Window Constraints (SPPTW), will be presented. The interaction of a ship with environmental influences – in our case wind, wave and ocean surface currents – will result in increasing or decreasing fuel consumption due to the ship's specific interaction with these forces which is described in Section 3.4 on fuel consumption calculation. As mentioned earlier, information on the weather data used is given in Section 3.5. Finally we will present the results from our computational test on the SPPTW (see Section 3.6).

3.1 Literature Review

Environmental routing can be subdivided into wave, ocean currents, wind and tides affected routing. There is little literature on maritime transportation problems discussing environmental routing problems. We will shortly summarize the most important literature on this topic in chronological order (see Table 3.1):

Two PhD theses extensively discuss ship routing under uncertainty and accordingly environmental routing are published by Hagiwara (1989) and Chen (1978). Hagiwara (1989) even includes the influence of sail assistance to vessels. While Chen (1978) allows for three different power settings, whereas Hagiwara calculates with a given average propeller revolution.

Papadakis and Perakis (1990) determine the minimal time route for vessels operating on short passages. With a variational calculus approach 44they were able to find a ship's power settings and routes, that would minimize travel time. This routing problem with stationary weather conditions has been extended to a problem considering time-dependent environmental conditions (Perakis and Papadakis 1989). Only considering wave heights and wave direction, they found out, that with the objective of finding the minimal transit time between two harbours, waiting for storms to pass is in no case an optimal strategy. With this time dependent approach, they were also able to calculate routes for longer distances and even for consecutive destination points.

A comparison between a stochastic and deterministic program to find the minimal fuel consuming path under ocean current influences has been described by Lo and McCord (1998) and McCord et al. (1999). Their stochastic formulation for eastbound voyages with the Gulf Stream outperformed the deterministic counterpart. On westbound voyages, against the current, both approaches performed equally well.

A problem with the objective to find the minimal sailing time for offshore yacht races has been described in Allsopp et al. (2000). They solved their problem with a stochastic dynamic programming algorithm under weather uncertainty for any two points on the ocean. Weather data accounted for are wind and ocean currents.

An approach that also uses stochastic dynamic programming has been presented by Azaron and Kianfar (2003). At the beginning of a voyage, weather information is assumed to be known for nodes close to the origin. In all other nodes an environmental variable is influencing the arc length as a random variable according to a continuous time Markov process. Which different weather data being accounted for has not been stated.

The influence of wind and waves on the choice of routes has been described in Montes (2005). With a modified Dijkstra algorithm the shortest path (shortest time) is determined. As examples, test results for the Pacific Ocean are shown.

An approach for finding a shortest path for unmanned aerial vehicles (UAVs) regarding wind as the environmental influence has been shown in Nachmani (2007). Several extensions to this model are given as stochastic-dynamic shortest path models, taking the stochastical behaviour of wind into consideration. The shortest time route or most economical route under consideration of wave data between two harbours has been solved by a Dijkstra algorithm by Padhy et al. (2008). Here, examples for routes in the Indian Ocean are calculated.

So far, to our knowledge, there exists no shortest path algorithm which takes wind, waves and ocean currents altogether into consideration and at the same time is applicable for different speed settings and alternative propulsion techniques as in our approach. An overview on the most relevant literature on environmental routing tasks is given in Table 3.1.

The construction of the underlying network can be carried out in several ways, upon which the shortest path algorithm can be applied (explained later in this section). The isochrone method, the N-Stage dynamic programming and the calculus of variation are three possible ways to construct the network. In the first two methods, the dynamic problem is discretised by splitting the continuous time span into time intervals. This can easily be done without loss to reality since ships usually adjust their power output and course only once or twice a day (Hagiwara 1989). The isochrone Method was originally developed by James (1957) to manually define the time minimal route. With this method a ship can reach multiple positions within a predefined time using different courses which are dependent on environmental influences (see Figure 3.1).

Author	Objective	Environmental data	Stochastic approach	Solution approach	Power / speed setting	Remarks
Chen (1978)	min cost	wind, waves	X	multi-stage dynamic stochastic programming algorithm	3 power settings	—
Hagiwara (1989)	min time/ fuel/ cost	wind, waves, ocean currents	X	modified Isochrone method	average propeller revolution	wind assisted propulsion possible
Perakis and Papadakis (1989)	min travel time	time dependent sea state	—	Calculus of variation	power setting variable	longer distances
Papadakis and Perakis (1990)	min travel time	sea state characteristic	—	Calculus of variation	constant power output	short passages
Lo and McCord (1998)	min fuel	ocean currents	X	stochastic dynamic programming	power setting variable	—
citeMccord1999	min fuel	ocean currents	—	dynamic programming	constant speed	2.5% average fuel saving
Allsopp et al. (2000)	max speed	wind, ocean currents	X	stochastic dynamic programming	— (sail boats)	for offshore yacht races
Azaron and Kianfar (2003)	shortest path	function of environmental variable	—	stochastic dynamic programming	constant power output	—
Montes (2005)	min travel time	wind, waves	—	modified Dijkstra SPP algorithm	constant speed	tested for western Pacific
Nachmani (2007)	min energy	wind	X	stochastic dynamic programming	variable speed	unmanned aerial vehicle (UAV)
Padhy et al. (2008)	min travel time	wave	-	modified Dijkstra SPP algorithm	optional speed reduction	tested for Indian Ocean

Table 3.1: Literature overview on environmental routing

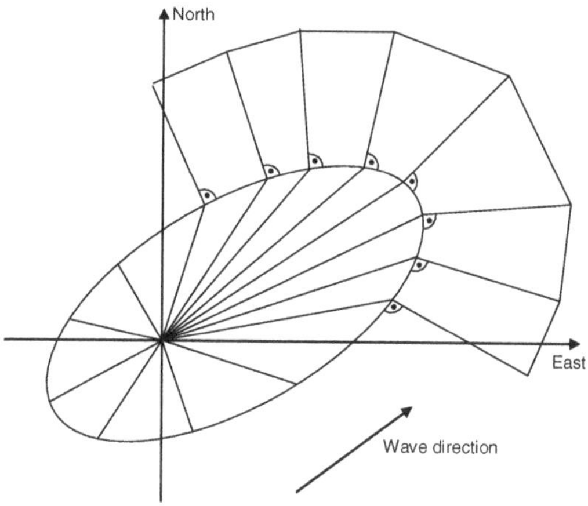

Figure 3.1: Constructing Isochrones, according to Szlapczynska and Smierzchalski (2007, p. 637)

An isochrone is the resulting line connecting all attainable positions. From various points of the first isochrone, new possible positions for the next time interval are created. Environmental influences on the construction of the isochrones are reflected by the elliptic shape of the isochrone (see Figure 3.1). Without environmental influences, the isochrone would result in a perfect circle. This procedure is repeated until the destination point is reached. To avoid unnecessary computing, the network construction is limited to a predefined area around the great circle route (see Figure 3.2). The figure illustrates a possible route from the origin X_0 to the destination point X_f. For each time interval $t_i \in t_0 \dots t_f$ isochrones X_i consists of k different points. The shortest path is now represented by the route which first reaches the destination point.

A modified version of the isochrone method, accounting for land mass along the desired route and avoiding so called closed isochrone loops is presented in Hagiwara (1989, p. 19-54).

For the dynamic programming approach a grid system is constructed for a feasible sailing region. Candidate way points represent the corners of these grid cells. For this type of network construction the resolution is important (Hagiwara 1989, p. 16). The size of each grid depends on the resolution of the available weather data, which in our case varies between 0.75° times 0.75°. Transforming the idea of Bellman (1957) to the dynamic programming of our ship routing problem, each subproblem consists of finding the shortest or minimal fuel path to each network point. Starting from the destination node,

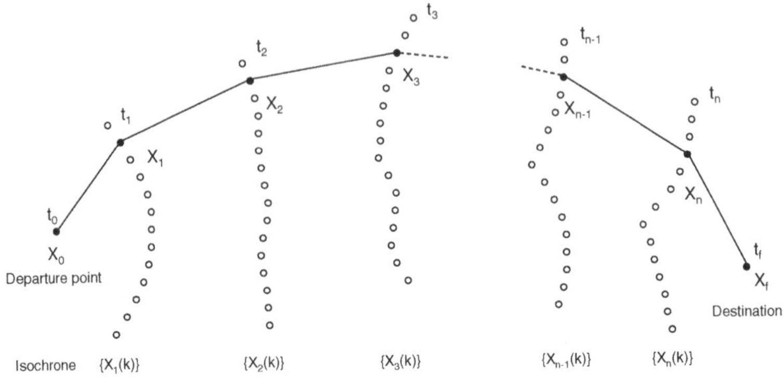

Figure 3.2: Constructing a network, according to (Hagiwara 1989, p. 24)

the optimal path to each network point is determined backwards. These results are saved for the ongoing calculation of shortest paths from that point to following points omitting redundant calculations. This again results in a network of nodes, for which not only the shortest path from the origin to the destination point is known, but also the shortest path from the origin to all nodes of the network.

Variational calculus, the analytical approach, applied to this maritime SPP, continuously and simultaneously considers the two parameters course and power output. The objective is to find the minimum cost route which is obtained by minimizing the integral that represents all environmental influences, at a given power output and time. For this approach all data needs to be continuous. Therefore the predominantly discrete data has to be transformed into continuous data. As mentioned above, the continuous adjustment of power output and course correction is not applicable in reality, therefore the use of this approach for environmental routing is not recommended.

3.2 SPP Network Design

A ship's crew, unlike a driver of a land-based vehicle that mainly travels on given roads or tracks, can navigate freely. Only in areas close to the shore, so called short sea, like the North and Baltic Sea or any canal, ships have to travel along predefined or regulated routes. However, on the open ocean there are no restrictions that limit the choice of routes for ships. Therefore we need an artificial network, for which a SPP can be formulated. In our approach we use a network design method similar to the one introduced by Lee et al. (2002). Here the benefits of the dynamic programming and the isochrone method are combined. The network reaches from the origin harbour to the destination harbour along a great circle route. From a centre point C , which is located at half the distance from the harbours, we turn 90° in a positive and negative direction from the direct course of the original great circle route. Along this new course direction, new centre points $C_{\pm i}$ are generated that are multiples of 60nm away from the centre point C (see Figure 3.4). A route along the outermost centre points spans the network in such a way, that a ship is still able to reach its destination harbour at maximum speed within the given time window. All other network points are on the great circle routes which connect the origin with the destination harbour going through the centre points. The network points on these great circle routes are again separated by a distance of 60nm. We took 60nm as distance for our network, since 1° of latitude has a length of about 60nm and for 1° longitude the same is true at least at the equator, with the distance being reduced to zero at the poles. The distance between two nodes of the network would allow a ship's crew to change the speed and course setting no more than roughly every 2.5 hours when travelling at an average speed of 23 kn. It increases to every 4 hours, when travelling at an average speed of 14 kn. An example of this network, connecting harbours Cadiz and New York - Newark can be seen in Figure 3.3.

From each point of the network three network arcs are generated, connecting the three closest network points. These three closest points have to be within ±60° in regard to the heading that one needs to reach the destination harbour of the regarded network point (see Figure 3.4). Only from the network point representing the origin harbour, all consecutive network points can be reached. This adds up to more than 3 arcs leaving the origin harbour network point.

In the strategic network design model, a ship has the choice of travelling at three different average speed settings between two harbours. These speed settings are: super slow steaming, slow steaming and a regular speed setting. Each of these strategic speed settings allow a ship to travel at three different possible speeds between two consecutive network points in our operational network. For super slow steaming we assume an average speed of 14kn, for slow steaming an average speed of 18kn and for the regular speed setting we calculate with an average speed setting of 23kn. For each of these speed settings we allow a speed variation of ±1kn in our operational SPP. For example in the slow steaming mode a ship can travel along a network arc at three different speeds from one network point to the next, these being 17 kn, 18 kn and 19 kn fast.

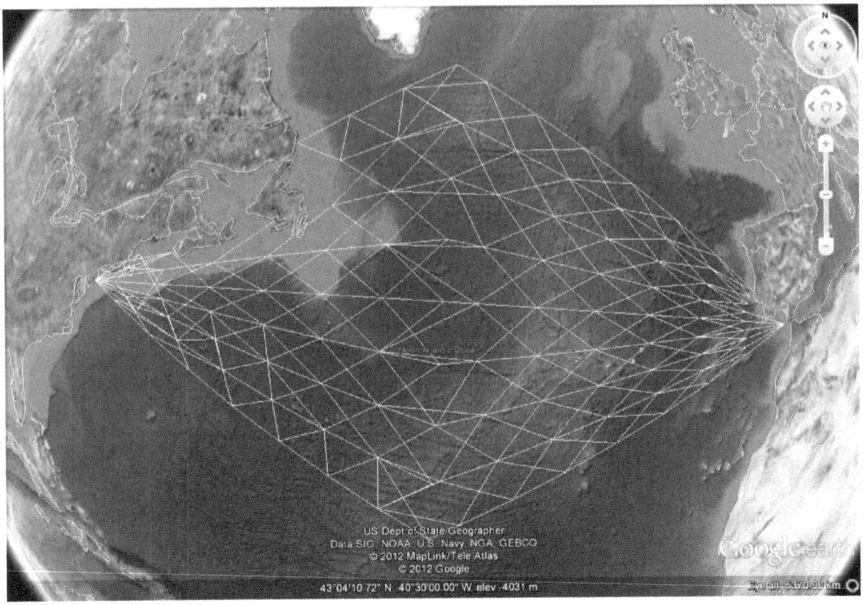

Figure 3.3: Example of a network connecting harbours Cadiz and New York - Newark, network displayed with Google Earth

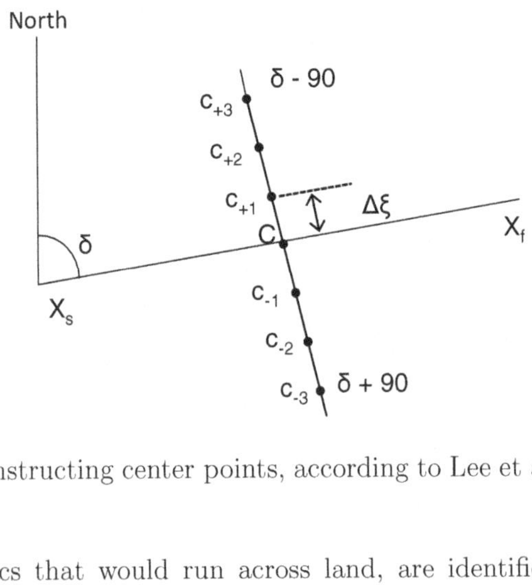

Figure 3.4: Constructing center points, according to Lee et al. (2002, p. 128)

Network arcs that would run across land, are identified based on the available weather data, since ocean currents and wave data are available for sea areas only. As the network has a different resolution than our weather

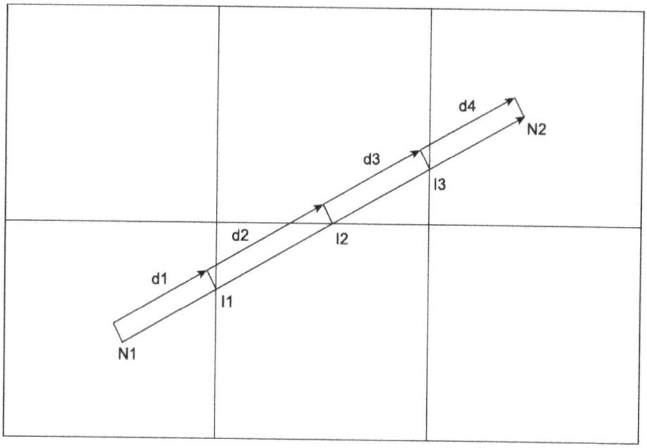

Figure 3.5: Creating interception arcs to given grid resolution

data, in most cases network arcs cross several different weather data grids (see Figure 3.5). To cope with this problem, all network arcs are divided into multiple smaller arcs, that represent the part of that network arc, which lies within a specific weather grid square. According to Figure 3.5, the network arc spans from point N_1 to N_2 . Each interception arc for example N_1 to I_1 or I_1 to I_2 has a different length, given for these examples with d_1 and d_2 in nm. The coordinates of all consecutive interception points of these smaller arcs, with $D_{I1,I2}$ the great circle distance measured in degree and $C_{I1,I2}$ the course between interception point $I1$ and $I2$, are calculated as shown in Figure 3.6.

$lat_{I2} = \arcsin(\sin(lat_{I1}) \cdot \cos(D_{I1,I2}) + \cos(lat_{I1}) \cdot \sin(D_{I1,I2}) \cdot \cos(C_{I1,I2}))$

if $(lat = 0)$ **then**

$lon_{I2} = lon_{I1}$

else

$$lon_{I2} = \left(lon_{I1} + \arcsin\left(\frac{\sin(C_{I1,I2}) * \sin(D_{I1,I2})}{\cos(lat_{I2}) + \pi}\right)\right) \quad \text{mod } 2\pi - \pi$$

end-if

Figure 3.6: Determination of course between interception point $I1$ and $I2$

In this case I_1 is the starting point of the interception arc and I_2 is the next point of the network arc to be obtained. With the resolution of the weather data being 0.75° time 0.75°, we know that the next interception point we are looking for has either a latitude with a multiple of 0.75°, a longitude with a multiple of 0.75°, or both. As we know the direction in which the ship will travel, we can now calculate the interception point with the smallest distance D_{I_1,I_2} to our current point on our course (see Figure 3.6). The great circle navigation formulas for calculating course and distance on a great circle are given in Appendix A.4. For each of these smaller arcs the fuel consumption, travel time and distances can now be calculated and summed up with all other smaller arcs, which then will represent the total travel time, fuel consumption and covered distance of the underlying network arc. This way even with a less dense resolution of the network detailed weather data information is not lost.

3.3 Shortest Path Problem

For our strategic network design, we want to compare the strategic networks created when using mean travelled distance, mean fuel consumed and mean travel time, obtained from a multi objective label-setting algorithm for the SPPTW with those received from using a modified Dijkstra algorithm for a general SPP. With the modified Dijkstra algorithm three different objectives are considered:

- minimum distance
- minimum travel time
- minimum fuel consumption

All three objectives are subject to a constant average speed the ship can travel at between these two harbours and to weather conditions of a given starting time. Due to the fact that an average speed is given, the resulting values of fuel consumed, travel time and travel distance are the same for the objectives minimum distance and minimum travel time.

A more challenging task is solving the SPPTW. For the use of a SPPTW for our case, the objective is to find a path along the network with minimal consumed fuel and to arrive at the destination harbour within a given time window. This time window is predefined as Latest Time of Arrival (LTA). As mentioned in the previous Section 3.2, the choice of selecting one of three different speeds for each arc of the network also has to be considered. The LTA is obtained by calculating the time needed when travelling on the great circle route from the origin to the destination harbour at the mean speed of the above mentioned three different speed choices. As an example for a ship travelling between the two harbours of Le Havre and Miami at an average speed of 18kn (corresponding to a slow steaming speed of our definition), the LTA would be obtained by dividing the great circle distance of 3879nm by 18kn, which gives us an LTA in Miami of about 216 hours or 9 days after leaving the departure harbour Le Havre. In our model formulation for the SPPTW the algorithm for solving the SPPTW can choose from three different speed settings. These three speed settings have values of the average speed setting and ±1kn, which in our example corresponds to 17kn, 18kn and 19kn. This freedom of choice is introduced, so that a ship has the possibility of circumnavigating bad weather conditions by either slowing down and wait for this weather to pass by or speeding up and pass that region before the weather gets worse. To solve this SPPTW we used an enhanced label-setting algorithm, that is introduced and explained in detail in the following.

For a general overview and classification of SPPs with Resource Constraints (SPPRC) the reader is referred to Irnich and Desaulniers (2005). The SPPTW with its two variable resources being time and costs, was first studied in Desrosiers et al. (1983, 1984), whereas the idea of label-setting algorithms is described in Ahuja et al. (1993).

Due to the choice of speed for each arc, a node $i \in V$ can be reached in many different ways. As soon as the label-setting algorithm has finished, and the destination harbour has been reached, we want to know which path was chosen by the algorithm. In order to be able to recall all visited network points along the path from the origin to the destination, each node i, that has been taken into account by the algorithm receives a set of labels L_i, which store all the needed information. In our case these are the fuel consumption C_i^p, the travel time T_i^p, the predecessor node of a label *pred*(L) and the speed v_p . C_i^p is the sum of all costs c_{ij} of arcs connecting nodes i and j along the chosen path p and T_i^p the sum of all travel times t_{ij}. v_p is the speed that has been selected on the arc connecting the last visited node with the current node i. Index p indicates the path of a set of paths P_i a node i can be reached with. The time windows are given with a_i and b_i, the earliest and latest arrival time. For each network node, the specific set of labels has to be sorted according to our objectives. Since we have two objectives, minimum fuel consumed at minimum travel time, we can apply a dominance rule. If label 1 has higher costs and longer travel time than label 2 ($(C_1, T_1) > (C_2, T_2)$), label 1 is said to be dominated by label 2 and can therefore be deleted from the set of labels L_i. If a label 1 has the same costs C_1 like another label 2 with C_2, but it has a shorter travel time T_1 than T_2 ($C_1 \geq C_2$, $T_1 \leq T_2$), label 1 dominates label 2 and again label 2 can therefore be deleted. If labels have the same values for costs and time, one can be neglected. This efficiency $Eff(L_i)$ of a set of labels can be formulated as shown in Equation 3.1.

$$Eff(L_i) = \{(C_i^p, T_i^p) \in L_i : \nexists (C_i^{p'}, T_i^{p'}) \in L_i, (C_i^{p'}, T_i^{p'}) \neq (C_i^p, T_i^k) \\ \text{with } (C_i^{p'}, T_i^{p'}) \leq (C_i^p, T_i^p)\} \quad (3.1)$$

With a lexikographical sorting, where criterion C^P is the first, we can now use a label-setting algorithm as described in Figure 4.8, that has been developed similar to Dijkstra's algorithm. In each iteration the label with the best values of costs and time is compared to all other labels and one of the temporarily marked labels is then selected to proceed with the algorithm. Similar to Dijkstra's approach, labels are distinguished in temporarily or permanently marked labels.

(Initialization) Set $L_s := \{(a_s, 0)\}$, $pred((a_s, 0)) = 0$,
$L_i = \emptyset$ for all i $\in V \backslash \{s\}$
(Loop) until $\bigcup_{i \in V} L_i \neq \emptyset$ is true, do:
(Selection) choose $(T_i, C_i) \in \bigcup_{i \in V} L_i$ with $(T_i, C_i) \overset{lex}{\leq} (T, C)$
 for all $(T, C) \in \bigcup_{i \in V} L_i$ (lexikographical minimum)
 set $L_i := L_i \setminus \{(T_i, C_i)\}$
 run through all successors $j \in \Delta^+(i)$ with $T_i + t_{ij} \leq b_j$:
  (Mark) set $(T_j, C_j) := (max\,\{a_j, T_i + t_{ij}\}, C_i + c_{ij}$
  $pred((T_j, C_j)) = (T_i, C_i)$
  $L_j := Eff(L_j \cup \{(T_j, C_j)\})$

Figure 3.7: Pseudo code according to Grünert and Irnich (2005, p. 297)

For a better understanding of the label-setting algorithm used for solving our SPPTW we will give a small example in the following. The network in Figure 3.3 displays nodes and directed arcs. On each arc a ship can travel at two different speed settings. From the start node 1 the ship can travel along any of the arcs and nodes to the destination node 11. To simulate weather dependent data, each arc has two costs, the higher costs for travelling at regular speed and the lesser one for travelling at reduced speed. Costs are given in cost unit per travelled nautical mile (nm). Even though the travel distance between two nodes might be equal, different costs will arise due to different weather conditions. Each node has an LTA which is calculated by subtracting the shortest time a ship could reach the destination node at highest possible speed from the LTA of destination node 11. As an example for node 5 , the LTA is calculated by subtracting 2.2 time periods from the latest time of arrival at the destination harbour which is 7 (see Figure 3.3 for example data). This results in 4.8 time periods being the LTA for node 5.

Starting at node 1, l_1 is the only label within the set of label L_1 has values 0 for costs, 0 for time consumed, no predecessor label and no speed setting selected ([0;0;-;-]). As each arc can be travelled on with two different speed settings, we end up with six labels after completing the first iteration, two for each node 2, 3 and 4, that can be visited from node 1 (see Figure 3.3).

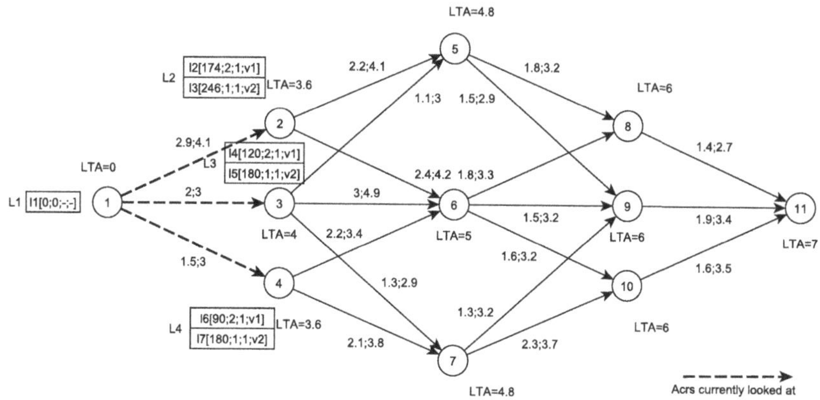

Figure 3.8: Label-setting example, step 1

For each node, none of the labels is dominated by another label and therefore we can not delete any labels. To further proceed with the next iteration we select the label with values $[90; 2; 1; v_1]$ at node 4, which has the lowest costs of all temporarily marked labels (see Figure 3.10). The time consumption is 2, the predecessor label is label l_1 (the starting label of node 1) and the selected speed for travelling from node 1 to node 4 is v_1, the lower speed setting.

After further iterations, labels l_{76} and l_{77} are generated for node 9 with a path, according to the predecessor labels, of 1-4-6-9 (see Figure 3.10). This is an example, where too much time is consumed when travelling on that path with a low speed setting, hence label l_{76} is deleted, since the time of arrival at node 9 is 6.3, which is larger then the LTA for node 9, being 6 time units. Label l_{77} with an arrival time of 5.3 still reaches the node within the given LTA.

	1	2	3	4	5	6	7	8	9	10	11
1		60 2 ; 1 2.9 ; 4.1	60 2 ; 1 2 ; 3	60 2 ; 1 1.5 ; 3	—	—	—	—	—	—	—
2	—		—	—	70 2.3 ; 1.2 2.2 ; 4.1	70 2.3 ; 1.2 2.4 ; 4.2	—	—	—	—	—
3	—	—		—	80 2.7 ; 1.3 1.1 ; 3	60 2 ; 1 3 ; 4.9	80 2.7 ; 1.3 1.3 ; 2.9	—	—	—	—
4	—	—	—		—	70 2.3 ; 1.2 2.2 ; 3.4	70 2.3 ; 1.2 2.1 ; 3.8	—		—	—
5	—	—	—	—		—	—	70 2.3 ; 1.2 1.8 ; 3.2	80 2.7 ; 1.3 1.5 ; 2.9	—	—
6	—	—	—	—	—		—	70 2.3 ; 1.2 1.8 ; 3.3	60 2 ; 1 1.5 ; 3.2	70 2.3 ; 1.2 1.6 ; 3.2	—
7	—	—	—	—	—	—		—	80 2.7 ; 1.3 1.3 ; 3.2	70 2.3 ; 1.2 2.3 ; 3.7	—
8	—	—	—	—	—	—	—		—	—	60 2 ; 1 1.4 ; 2.7
9	—	—	—	—	—	—	—	—		—	60 2 ; 1 1.9 ; 3.4
10	—	—	—	—	—	—	—	—	—		60 2 ; 1 1.6 ; 3.5
11	—	—	—	—	—	—	—	—	—	—	

Distance
travel times
consumption

Figure 3.9: Example data

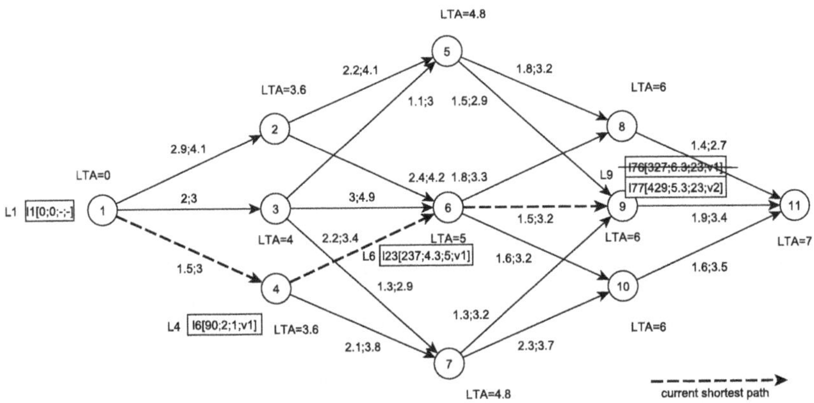

Figure 3.10: Labelsetting example, further iteration steps

The overall optimal solution for this example network can be seen in Figure 3.11. From all generated labels of the destination node 11, label l_{131} is selected, having minimum costs and an arrival time of 7. The lexicographic

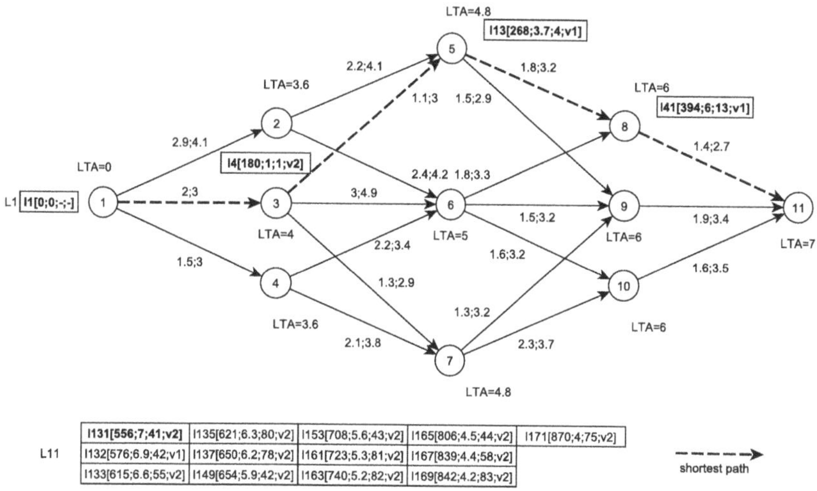

Figure 3.11: Label-setting example, optimal solution

optimal path therefore results in visiting nodes 1, 3, 5, 8 and finally 11. As one can see, the speed setting is not always the lowest possible. On the arc connecting label 1 and 3 for example, a ship would have to travel with the higher speed setting to be able to reach the destination within the given LTA of 7 time units.

3.4 Calculation of Ship Fuel Consumption

Since the effect of environmental influences on the strategic liner shipping network design is going to be examined in a subsequent chapter, the fuel consumed on routes between all considered harbours has to be calculated depending on varying seasonal environmental influences. Predicting a ships behaviour encountering wind, waves and currents via simulation models is still a great challenge for research in the field of marine engineering (Conference 2008). The following modelling approaches are not the state of the art, but have been discussed intensively in recent years and allow for a good approximation of the ships motions. In our case an exact prediction of the ships resistance is not considered. We are more interested in showing that for example a ship of a larger size or a ship in bad weather conditions has more resistance than a smaller ship or the same ship in in fair weather conditions. Especially the disproportional rise of fuel consumption with increasing speed is well reproduced with ship modelling techniques shown below.

Environmental influences that interact with a ship while travelling on oceans are the water resistance, the resistance due to ocean currents and the wind resistance, which will be introduced in the following. The water resistance is further divided into a calm water resistance and a resistance resulting from waves. Additionally, we will present a formula that represents the possible propulsion force of kite sailing systems. Several different alternative propulsion techniques have been presented recently. A prototype ship taking its energy from waves has crossed the pacific from Hawaii to Japan in 2008 (Horie 2011). Boat and ships exclusively receiving its energy from solar power have only been designed for recreational purposes (Kopf 2011; PlanetSolar 2011, see e.g.). To be able to drive a ship solely by solar power, the amount of solar panels and their needed space would be too large to effectively propel freight ships. For freight ships, solar power can only be used as an additional energy source. As an example the Auriga Leader is a car carrier, that only receives up to 1% of the needed propulsion power from solar panels installed on the deck of the ship (NYK 2009). We believe that a wind dependent propulsion system such as a kite (see SkySails 2011) or a Flettner rotor (see Enercon 2010) are most promising. Therefore we decided to concentrate only on kite propulsion systems as an additional propulsion system.

According to their lesser importance we do not account for the draught and trim of a ship that varies depending on the amount of cargo and fuel loaded. For the same reason, the fouling of the ships hull and propeller is also not considered.

Water Resistance

The calculation of water resistance as shown in the following, is the resistance that acts on a ship when travelling through calm water without any kind of wave interaction. The calm water resistance R_T is the sum of the wave making resistance, the friction resistance and the viscous pressure resistance which is derived as shown in equation (3.2) (Schneekluth and Betram 1998, p 185). Where C_T is the total drag coefficient, ρ_{SW} the density of sea water (SW), V_S the ship's velocity and A_S the wetted surface area of a ship's hull.

$$R_T = \frac{C_T \cdot \rho_{SW} \cdot V_S^2 \cdot A_S}{2} \tag{3.2}$$

Usually the resistance of ships is calculated upon coefficients obtained from towing tank tests of model ships. With these coefficients the resistance performance of the original size ship is represented. C_T, usually obtained from towing tank experiments, represents a total drag coefficient which is the sum of the friction coefficient C_F and the remaining drag coefficient C_R.

$$C_T = C_F + C_R \tag{3.3}$$

The friction coefficient C_F is calculated according to the proceedings of the ITTC (International Towing Tank Conference) by the following approximation (Hughes 1957, p. 220).

$$C_F = \frac{0.075}{(\log(Re) - 2)^2} \tag{3.4}$$

The Reynold number Re is obtained from the ratio of speed V_S and length L of the ship as well as the kinematic viscosity ν of sea water.

$$Re = \frac{V_S \cdot L}{\nu} \tag{3.5}$$

The analytical definition of the remaining drag coefficient C_R is due to its complex physical interrelation usually determined by towing tank test. Thereby the proportion of speed and ships' length has to be the same for the towing test model as for the real size ship. This way the remaining drag coefficient is valid for both ships. Froude's number F_N is used as a performance figure, defined by the fraction of the ship's speed V_S and the square root of the ship's length L times the earth's gravity g :

$$F_N = \frac{V_S}{\sqrt{g \cdot L}} \tag{3.6}$$

To spare towing tests for each type of ship, a function approximating the remaining drag coefficient has been developed, which has been created from numerous towing tests (Schneekluth 1988, p. 495).

$$C_R = \frac{(10F_N - 0.8)^4 \cdot (10C_P - 3.3)^2 \cdot (10^3 C_\nabla + 4) \cdot 0.0012}{10^3} + \frac{+50C_\nabla + (\frac{B}{T} - 2.5) \cdot 0.17 + 0.2}{10^3} \tag{3.7}$$

All factors are subject to bounds as shown in Table 3.2, where the left hand side indicates the lower bound and the right hand side the upper bound of the values possible range.

To receive values for the volume-length coefficient C_∇ , the prismatic coefficient C_P and the Ayre block coefficient $C_{B,AYRE}$, which belongs to

F_N		C_∇		C_P		C_B	L/B	
0.17	0.3	0.011	2	0.5	0.8	$< C_{B,AYRE}+0.06$	5	10

Table 3.2: Value constraints for remaining drag coefficient approximation function (Schneekluth 1988, p. 495)

single screw ships and depending on the ship's Length L, breadth B, draught T and displacement ∇, following equations are used:

$$C_\nabla = \frac{\nabla}{L^3} \tag{3.8}$$

$$C_P = \frac{\nabla}{L \cdot B \cdot T \cdot C_M} \tag{3.9}$$

$$C_{B,AYRE} = 1.08 - 1.68 \cdot F_N \tag{3.10}$$

The mid ship section area coefficient for the towing tank tests C_M equals 0.926. To approximate the wetted surface area A_S the following approach has been chosen (Danckwardt 1969, p. 124):

$$A_S = \frac{\nabla}{B} \cdot \left[\frac{1.7}{C_B - 0.2 \cdot (C_B - 0.65)} + \frac{B}{T}\right] \tag{3.11}$$

Wind Resistance

Wind is a factor which directly influences the routing of a ship. The apparent wind blows against the ship's above water surface A_{AWS} , which consists of the ship's hull above water, the superstructure such as housing and bridge and all cargo above the hull. The apparent wind V_{AW} is determined by the fair wind V_{FW} which has the opposite direction but same speed as the ship and the true wind V_{TW}, which can be measured at a fixed point in the same region. Both, the resulting apparent wind velocity and direction have to be determined in order to receive the wind resistance.

γ_W is the angle between the direction of motion and the apparent wind. With β_W being the angle between the true wind and the fair wind (see Figure 3.12), the velocity of the apparent wind can be obtained by:

$$V_{AW} = \sqrt{V_{TW}^2 + V_{FW}^2 - 2 \cdot V_{TW} \cdot V_{FW} \cdot \cos(\beta_W)} \tag{3.12}$$

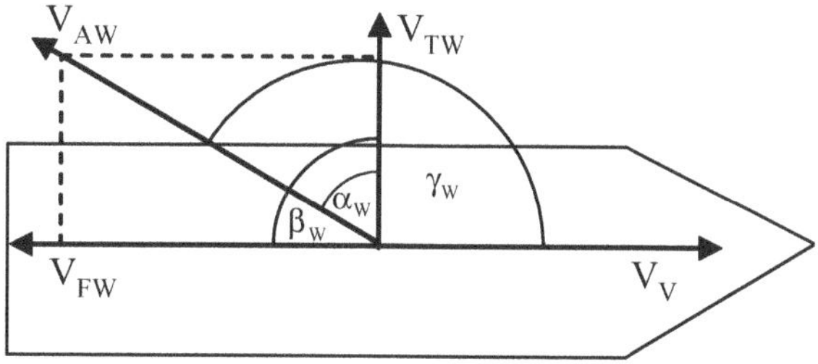

Figure 3.12: Wind directions and angles according to ships heading

The angle α_W between the apparent wind direction and the true wind direction can be calculated as follows:

$$\alpha_W = 2 \cdot \arcsin\left(\sqrt{\frac{(s - V_{AW}) \cdot (s - V_{FW})}{V_{AW} \cdot V_{FW}}}\right),$$

$$\text{with s} = \frac{V_{AW} + V_{FW} + V_{TW}}{2} \tag{3.13}$$

With the above mentioned equations (3.12) and (3.13) the wind resistance R_W can now be obtained. Since only the portion of the apparent wind blowing in the ship's travel direction influences the wind resistance, the function depends on the incidence angle γ_W between the apparent wind and the ship'sf heading.

$$R_W = \cos(\gamma_W) \cdot c_W \cdot \frac{\rho_A \cdot V_{AW}^2}{2} \cdot A_{AWS} \tag{3.14}$$

Again A_{AWS} also depends on the incident angle of the apparent wind. The above water surface of the ship is the resulting surface in the opposite direction of the apparent wind direction.

Wave Resistance

Ships are slowed down by resistance caused by higher waves. The waves, or so called sea state, mainly depend on the strength of the wind. That kind of resistance has an especially high influence on a ship at a small wave height ζ and a ship length ($\frac{\zeta}{L} < 1$) (Yaozong 1989) on which weather a ship can travel without significant oscillation. At higher waves and lengths, the ship starts moving around its yaw, roll and pitch axis. These movements of course are highly dependent on the travelling direction of the ship and the impacting mean wave direction. As pitching is mainly influenced by waves coming from the front and lateral or abaft incoming waves result in rolling of the ship. Steering against yawing movements also yields additional resistance. As already mentioned for the pure water resistance, analytical results from towing tests are again the basis for our calculation of the wave resistance. Moor and Murdy (1968) have collected measurements for 34 different ship models with a length between 16 and 18 ft, for wave heights of five to eight Beaufort. From these results they developed a function to predict the additional wave resistance for real size ships.

For our calculations the dimensionless additional wave resistance $R_{sea,MM}$ depending on the calm water resistance R_T is obtained as follows:

$$\begin{aligned} R_{sea,MM} = A_0 + A_1 \cdot (C_B - 0.5)^5 + A_2 \cdot \frac{L}{B} + A_3 \cdot \frac{L}{T} + \\ A_4 \cdot LCB + A_5 \cdot \frac{k_{yy}}{L} + A_6 \cdot \frac{V}{\sqrt{L}} \end{aligned} \tag{3.15}$$

The coefficients $A_0 - A_6$ for our ship types used are listed in Table A.2 in Appendix A.2. k_{yy} is the longitudinal radius of gyration about an axis through the centre of gravity and LCB the longitudinal position of centre of buoyancy from midships. Since the method of Moor and Murdy (1968) is only valid for wave heights between five and eight Beaufort, we need another approach for the wave height interval between 0 and 4 Beaufort (the wave height mainly depends on the force of the wind). A good method is the one described by Kreitner (1939). With this method the additional wave resistance $R_{sea,K}$ is obtained as follows:

$$R_{sea,K} = \frac{B}{T} \cdot \left(0.8 \cdot \frac{\zeta}{L}\right)^2 \tag{3.16}$$

Since the values of both methods' gradients do not match at a wave height of 5, measured in Beaufort '(Bn), we obtain values for wave height smaller than $\zeta < 1.5m$ in the following manner:

$$R_{sea}(\zeta < 1.5m) = R_{sea,K} \cdot \frac{R_{sea,MM}(Bn = 5) \cdot R_T}{R_{sea,K}(\zeta_W = 1.5m)} \tag{3.17}$$

With this continuous gradient we are now able to calculate the wave resistance for different speed settings and wave heights of waves coming from the front. But as mentioned earlier, wave resistance depends on the incidence angle of the waves. For this we use a method of Yaozong (1989) (p. 19-20) which gives us a factor that only needs to be multiplied with our wave resistance obtained from the approaches of Moor and Murdy (1968) and Kreitner (1939) '(see also Figure A.2 in Appendix A.3). This factor depends on the incidence angle of the waves and is scaled between 0 and 1. Waves coming from the front (180°) have a factor of 100% and those coming from the rear have the lowest value of approximately 20%.

Current Resistance

Ocean surface currents cause a shift of the ship in relation to the sea floor. To compensate this shift, the ship's course and speed have to be adapted to hold the desired ground speed and direction. To account for the additional or saved amount of fuel caused by currents, the speed setting is computed as follows:

$$V_C = \sqrt{V_{CU}^2 + V_{CO}^2 - 2 \cdot V_{CU} \cdot V_{CO} \cdot \cos(\alpha_C U)} \tag{3.18}$$

V_{CU} is the ocean current velocity. V_{CO} is the desired velocity of the ship over ground in course direction. The angle α_{CU} indicates the angle between the direction of the ocean current and the ship's desired course. The resulting speed is entered into the formula (3.2) for calculating a ship's water resistance.

Kite Propulsion Force

The kite propulsion force is estimated from publicly available information (see SkySails 2011). The propulsion force R_K is the sum of two components (see Equation 3.19). The first component $R_{KD}(\gamma_{AW})$ depends on the direction and the second $R_{KV}(V_{AW})$ on the speed of the apparent wind (AW). As shown in Figure 3.13 the kite only operates within 50° to 310° in relation to the apparent wind direction.

$$R_K = R_{KD}(\gamma_{AW}) + R_{KV}(V_{AW}) \tag{3.19}$$

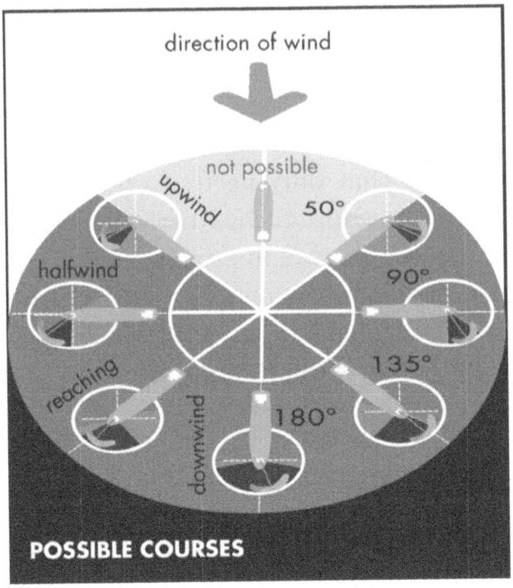

Figure 3.13: SkySails, possible courses (SkySails 2009)

To estimate the kite force that depends on the direction of the apparent wind, following function is used:

$$R_{KD} = a + b \cdot \cos(\gamma_{AW}) + c \cdot \cos(2 \cdot \gamma_{AW}) + d \cdot \cos(3 \cdot \gamma_{AW}) \tag{3.20}$$

Constants a, b, c and d are given and they depend on the kite's size. Details on all input data can be found in Appendix A.1. The kite of such systems is flown through the air in a way comparable to an eight shaped manoeuvre. The wind velocity dependent component of the kites propulsion force R_{KV} is therefore calculated as follows:

$$R_{KV} = \sin(\gamma_P) \cdot c_W \cdot \frac{\rho_A \cdot V_T^2}{2} \cdot A_K \tag{3.21}$$

γ_P indicates the pitch angle of the kite flying above the ship with a wind resistance coefficient c_W. ρ_A is the density of air and A_K the size of the kite given in m^2. Due to the eight shaped flight, the tip velocity V_T of the kite is the multiple (2.68 in our case) of the apparent wind velocity. A figure describing the kite propulsion force gradient according to the direction of the apparent wind is shown in Figure A.1 of Appendix A.1.

Fuel Consumption

All of the above mentioned influences, the wind, water and wave resistance as well as the wind propulsion, are now combined to receive the fuel consumption curve of a specific ship type under environmental influences. To overcome these combined resistances R_G, a ship needs to apply a corresponding power output. The ship's speed (V_s) dependent brake power (P_B) can be obtained as follows:

$$P_B = \frac{R_G \cdot V_s}{\eta_D \cdot \eta_S} \tag{3.22}$$

Where η_D and η_S are the efficiency of propulsion and transmission respectively and R_G subsuming all of the above mentioned resistances:

$$\begin{aligned} R_G = R_T(V_W, T, \nabla) + R_W(\gamma_W, V_{AW}) + \\ R_{sea}(\zeta_W, V_K, R_T, T) - R_K(\gamma_W, V_{AW}) \end{aligned} \tag{3.23}$$

To now receive the amount of fuel consumed, we use a function as proposed by Perakis and Jaramillo (1991, p. 197).

$$FC = (a_k \cdot P_b)^{b_k} + BC_k \tag{3.24}$$

a_k and b_k in our case are ship type k dependent coefficients and BC_k is its corresponding base consumption (for ship dependent values see Appendix A.2). The base consumption is the amount of fuel consumed by a ship when for instance being in a harbour for loading or unloading.

3.5 Weather Data

Wind and wave data have been provided by the DWD (Deutscher Wetterdienst), the german governmental weather services. These data include wind and wave data for longitudes ranging from 0° to 359.25° and latitudes between -72° south and 72° north, both with a 0.75° spacing. The time spans over a whole year starting on January 1st 2009 until December 31st 2009, with a 3 hour resolution. This leads to eight data sets per day. Wind speed is given in metres per second at 10m altitude, wind direction in degrees. The wave encountered in a specific region depends on wind generated waves and swell, where the wind generated waves are called wind sea. Swell are waves which originally are created by wind but are observed in regions far away from their origin. So when no wind is blowing in a region but waves are observed, these waves are called swell. For our calculation of ship behaviour on waves, we take into account the given significant wave height, given in meters, which is the resulting wave height from wind sea and swell. The other two parameters that have influence on a ship when encountering waves are the frequency and direction of the waves. For better computational performance we assume that the direction of the wind waves is the most dominant direction of all wave types and therefore consider these as our wave direction input data measured in degrees. The frequency of waves is given as a peak-period measured in seconds, which is the time between two consecutive peak waves observed at a stationary point. Again we adopt the peak-period of wind sea for our calculations. We received the ocean current data from MyOcean. The time resolution of these data is 1 week. Due to too little fluctuation compared to wind and waves, this is sufficiently precise. MyOcean is a three year project funded by the European Commission as part of the 7th Framework Program for European Research and Development. With this program a European capacity for Global Monitoring for Environment and Security (GMES) has been established. The current data we received (GLOBAL_REANALYSIS_PHYS_001_003_b) are given in a Mercator projection where the longitudal step is kept constant at 1/3 and the latitude varies in degree but is constant in km (for further explanation see Rosmorduc et al. 2011). All data from both sources are reanalysis data. Reanalysis in meteorology is a modern analysis or forecast model on historical weather data. Weather data is not collected for wide areas of the oceans. Therefore data is always predicted for those areas. These predictions or forecast models change over time and improve constantly. Newer models are hence also used to improve the accuracy of historical data. This process is called a reanalysis. In our case, the weather data of the year 2009 has been newly forecasted in the year 2011 with state of the art forecasting models. The underlying weather data is not regarded as static input based on the time of leaving the departure harbour. With increasing travel time our algorithm uses the weather data of the position and the time interval the ship is currently at. Hence, the weather data being closest time and region wise is taken as the basis for calculating the fuel consumption.

3.6 Computational Tests

In this section we analyse the label-setting algorithm that we use to solve our environmental routing problem which, as described earlier, can be defined as a SPPTW. Costs in our case represent the fuel consumed by a ship travelling from one to another node of the network. Due to the enormous size of the resulting SPP, we limited the amount of possible speed settings a ship can take between two consecutive nodes to three.

As an example, the number of labels generated when travelling from the harbour of Le Havre to the harbour of Miami, adds up to 100,034 on a network with spacing of 60nm (see Figure 3.15, left side). For this network setting a ship of type Rafaela would consume 243t of fuel and would travel for 260 hours at an average speed of 14kn on a 3,879nm long path. On a network with an extended spacing of network nodes to 240nm the same ship would consume 242t of fuel and would travel 255 hours again at an average speed of 14kn on a 3,878nm long path (see Figure 3.15, right side). Both ships' voyages where calculated with April 1st 2009 as starting time at harbour Le Havre. This shows that a greater spacing does not necessarily lead to inferior results compared to a higher network resolution. The benefit of networks with lower resolution is that they need less computational time. The number of labels needed for the same connection (Le Havre to Miami) drops to 2,629 labels for the 240nm network resolution which is only 2.6% of the amount of labels used for the 60nm network resolution. A computation on a single thread of an Intel Core2 Duo processor with 2.4 GHz clock speed and 3GB RAM only needs 169,478 ms for the 240nm network resolution compared to 5,030,875 ms for the 60nm resolution network which is a 96.6% reduction in computational time for this example.

To further reduce the computational time, we reduced the network point spacing to 120nm for harbours with a great circle distance of more than 1,500nm and less than 3,000nm. For those harbour connections with a great circle distance of more than 3,000nm, we set the network point spacing to 240nm. Even with a spacing that large, a ship crew will change the course and speed settings roughly every 17 hours, at an average speed of 14 kn. This is still in conformance with the statement of Hagiwara (1989) that a crew changes speed and course settings only once or twice a day.

In our example we used 6 ships of different hull size, cargo carrying capacity and engine power (see Table A.2 in Appendix A.2). These ships can be operated with or without an alternative kite propulsion, which gives a total of 12 different types of ship settings. According to the SPPTW we have to calculate the fuel consumed when travelling between two harbours for all ship types. The distances, travel time, and fuel consumptions of all ship types has been computed for every relation of the 33 harbours in the Gulf of Mexico, North Atlantic and North Sea (for a list of all harbours see Table 3.3).

Due to the fact that ships cannot freely manoeuvre in short-sea (coastal)

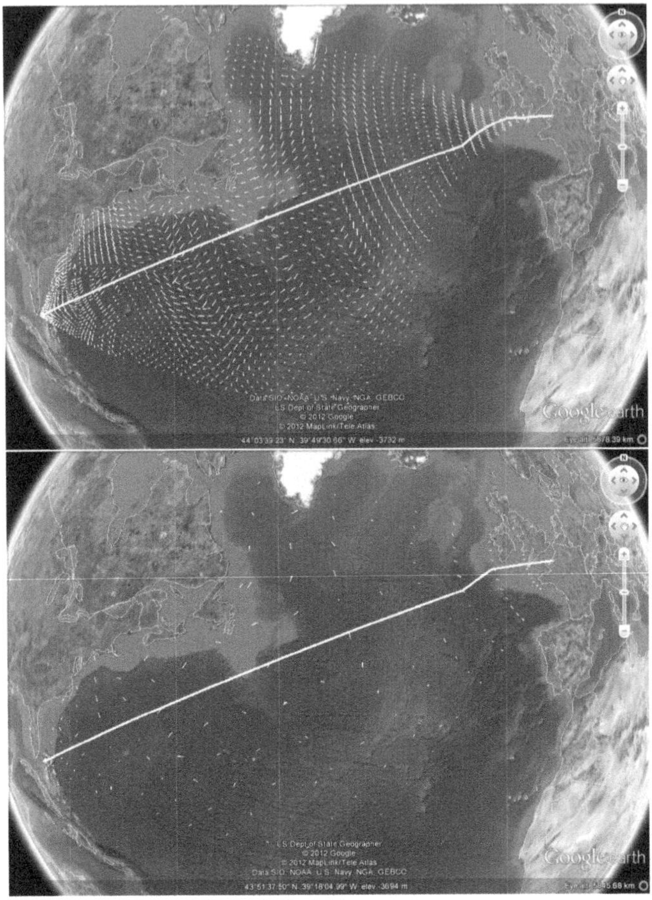

Figure 3.14: SPPTW from Le Havre to Miami network with resolution of 60nm (top) and resolution of 240nm (bottom), displayed with Google Earth.

regions like the English Channel or along coastal lines, harbours located very close to each other were not separately calculated by solving the SPPTW algorithm, but received the same values for routes to far distant harbours. Harbours where a seperate calculation is not warranted due to their short distance between them are for example Sines and Lisbon or Cadiz and Tangier / Algeciras. This means that for example the calculated values for distance, fuel consumption and travel time are the same for harbour connections Lisbon – Miami / Port Everglades and Sines – Miami / Port Everglades. All such harbour to harbour relations are marked by number 4 in Table 3.4.

Harbour	Region	Ocean \Sea
Manzanillo	Panama	Gulf of Mexico
Puerto Moin	Costa Rica	Gulf of Mexico
Fort-de-France	Martinique	Gulf of Mexico
Pointre-à-Pitre	Guadeloupe	Gulf of Mexico
Kingston	Jamaica	Gulf of Mexico
Veracruz	Mexico	Gulf of Mexico
Altamira	Mexico	Gulf of Mexico
Houston	USA	Gulf of Mexico
New Orleans	USA	Gulf of Mexico
Mobile	USA	Gulf of Mexico
Miami \Port Everglades	USA	North Atlantic
Freeport	Bahamas	North Atlantic
Savannah \Charleston	USA	North Atlantic
Jacksonville	USA	North Atlantic
Norfolk	USA	North Atlantic
Philadelphia	USA	North Atlantic
New York \Newark	USA	North Atlantic
Halifax	Canada	North Atlantic
Montreal	Canada	North Atlantic
Tangier \Algeciras	Morocco \Spain	North Atlantic
Cadiz	Spain	North Atlantic
Sines	Portugal	North Atlantic
Lisbon	Portugal	North Atlantic
Montoir-de-Bretagne	France	North Atlantic
Liverpool	Great Britain	North Atlantic
Le Havre	France	North Atlantic
Southampton	Great Britain	North Sea
Thames Port \Tilbury	Great Britain	North Sea
Felixstowe	Great Britain	North Sea
Dunkerque	France	North Sea
Antwerp	Belgium	North Sea
Rotterdam	Netherlands	North Sea
Bremerhaven	Germany	North Sea

Table 3.3: List of all 33 harbours considered.

An example for harbours linked by fixed routes in a short sea area are the harbours near the English Channel like Antwerp, Bremerhaven, Dunkerque, Felixtowe, Southampton and Rotterdam. For routes from a more distant harbour, we took values from Le Havre and added to those fixed distances, speed dependent travel times and fuel consumptions. These fixed values have been calculated by computing shortest distance problems without environmental influences. In Table 3.4 these harbour connections are marked by number 1.

Additionally, harbours that cannot be accessed directly because of natural barriers, are linked to other harbours via additional way points. Those harbours are for example all harbours within the Gulf of Mexico and harbours in Europe. For harbours within the Gulf of Mexico, Miami / Port Everglades is taken as a transit point that all ships have to pass when travelling eastward. This has the positive effect that SPPs only have to be solved for relations to and from Miami / Port Everglades, so further reducing the computing effort. These connections are marked by number 3 in Table 3.4. By these three simplifications a total of 1,056 $(33 \cdot 32)$ harbour relations that would have to be solved by a SPPTW, reduces to 249 harbour relations marked with number 2 in Table 3.4.

Table 3.4: Harbour to harbour connections

To \ From	Altamira	Antwerp	Bremerhaven	Cadiz	Dunkerque	Felixstowe	Fort de France	Freeport	Halifax	Houston	Jacksonville	Kingston	Le Havre	Lisbon	Liverpool	Manzanillo	Miami / Port Everglades	Mobile	Montoir de Bretagne	Montreal	New Orleans	New York / Newark	Norfolk	Philadelphia	Pointe-A-Pitre	Puerto Moin	Rotterdam	Savannah / Charleston	Sines	Southampton	Tangier / Algericas	Thames Port / Tilbury	Veracruz
Altamira	-	3	3	3	3	3	3	3	3	1	3	**2**	3	3	3	**2**	**2**	**2**	3	3	**2**	3	3	3	3	1	3	3	4	3	4	3	1
Antwerp	3	-	1	3	1	1	3	3	3	3	3	3	1	3	1	3	3	3	3	3	3	3	3	3	3	3	1	3	3	1	3	1	3
Bremerhaven	3	1	-	3	1	1	3	3	3	3	3	3	1	3	1	3	3	3	3	3	3	3	3	3	3	3	1	3	3	1	3	1	3
Cadiz	3	3	3	-	3	3	**2**	4	**2**	3	**2**	**2**	3	1	3	3	**2**	3	3	3	3	**2**	**2**	**2**	**2**	3	3	**2**	1	3	1	3	3
Dunkerque	3	1	1	3	-	1	3	3	3	3	3	3	1	3	1	3	3	3	3	3	3	3	3	3	3	3	1	3	3	1	3	1	3
Felixstowe	3	1	1	3	1	-	3	3	3	3	3	3	1	3	1	3	3	3	3	3	3	3	3	3	3	3	1	3	3	1	3	1	3
Fort de France	3	3	3	**2**	3	3	-	3	3	3	3	1	**2**	**2**	**2**	**2**	3	3	**2**	3	3	3	3	3	1	**2**	3	3	4	3	4	3	3
Freeport	3	3	3	4	3	3	3	-	**2**	3	**2**	1	4	4	4	**2**	1	3	4	3	3	**2**	**2**	**2**	**2**	**2**	3	1	4	3	4	3	3
Halifax	3	3	3	**2**	3	3	3	**2**	-	3	**2**	**2**	**2**	**2**	**2**	**2**	**2**	3	**2**	1	3	1	**2**	**2**	**2**	**2**	3	**2**	4	3	4	3	3
Houston	1	3	3	3	3	3	3	3	3	-	3	**2**	3	3	3	**2**	**2**	1	3	3	1	3	3	3	3	**2**	3	3	4	3	4	3	**2**
Jacksonville	3	3	3	**2**	3	3	3	**2**	**2**	3	-	3	**2**	**2**	**2**	**2**	**2**	3	**2**	3	3	**2**	1	**2**	**2**	**2**	3	1	4	3	4	3	3
Kingston	**2**	3	3	**2**	3	3	1	1	**2**	**2**	3	-	**2**	**2**	**2**	**2**	4	**2**	**2**	3	**2**	**2**	3	3	**2**	**2**	3	**2**	4	3	4	3	**2**
Le Havre	3	1	1	3	1	1	**2**	3	**2**	3	**2**	**2**	-	1	1	3	**2**	3	1	3	3	**2**	**2**	**2**	**2**	3	1	**2**	3	1	3	1	3
Lisbon	3	3	3	1	3	3	**2**	4	**2**	3	**2**	**2**	1	-	**2**	3	**2**	3	**2**	**2**	3	**2**	**2**	**2**	**2**	3	3	**2**	1	3	1	1	3
Liverpool	3	1	1	3	1	1	**2**	4	**2**	3	**2**	**2**	1	1	-	3	**2**	3	1	3	3	**2**	**2**	**2**	**2**	3	3	**2**	3	1	3	1	3
Manzanillo	**2**	3	3	3	3	3	**2**	**2**	**2**	**2**	3	**2**	3	3	3	-	4	**2**	3	3	**2**	**2**	**2**	**2**	**2**	1	3	3	4	3	4	3	1
Miami / Port Everglades	**2**	3	3	**2**	3	3	3	1	**2**	4	**2**	**2**	**2**	**2**	**2**	4	-	1	**2**	3	1	**2**	**2**	**2**	**2**	**2**	3	1	4	3	4	3	**2**
Mobile	**2**	3	3	3	3	3	3	3	3	1	3	**2**	3	3	3	**2**	**2**	-	3	3	1	3	3	3	**2**	**2**	3	3	4	3	4	3	**2**
Montoir de Bretagne	3	3	3	3	3	3	**2**	4	**2**	3	**2**	**2**	1	1	1	3	**2**	3	-	3	3	**2**	**2**	**2**	**2**	3	3	**2**	3	1	1	1	3
Montreal	3	3	3	**2**	3	3	3	3	1	3	3	3	3	**2**	**2**	3	3	3	**2**	-	3	3	3	3	3	3	3	3	4	3	4	3	3
New Orleans	**2**	3	3	3	3	3	3	3	3	1	3	**2**	3	3	3	**2**	**2**	1	3	3	-	3	3	3	**2**	**2**	3	3	4	3	4	3	**2**
New York / Newark	3	3	3	**2**	3	3	3	**2**	1	3	**2**	**2**	**2**	**2**	**2**	**2**	**2**	3	**2**	3	3	-	1	1	**2**	**2**	3	1	4	3	4	3	3
Norfolk	3	3	3	**2**	3	3	3	**2**	**2**	3	1	**2**	**2**	**2**	**2**	**2**	**2**	3	**2**	3	3	1	-	1	**2**	**2**	3	1	4	3	4	3	3
Philadelphia	3	3	3	**2**	3	3	3	**2**	**2**	3	**2**	**2**	**2**	**2**	**2**	**2**	**2**	3	**2**	3	3	1	1	-	**2**	**2**	3	1	4	3	4	3	3
Pointe-A-Pitre	3	3	3	**2**	3	3	1	**2**	**2**	3	**2**	**2**	**2**	**2**	**2**	**2**	**2**	**2**	**2**	3	**2**	**2**	**2**	**2**	-	**2**	3	**2**	4	3	4	3	**2**
Puerto Moin	1	3	3	3	3	3	**2**	**2**	**2**	**2**	3	**2**	3	3	3	1	**2**	**2**	3	3	**2**	**2**	**2**	**2**	**2**	-	3	3	3	3	4	3	1
Rotterdam	3	1	1	3	1	1	3	3	3	3	3	3	1	3	3	3	3	3	3	3	3	3	3	3	3	3	-	3	3	3	3	1	3
Savannah / Charleston	3	3	3	**2**	3	3	3	1	**2**	3	1	3	**2**	**2**	**2**	**2**	1	3	**2**	3	3	1	1	1	**2**	**2**	3	-	4	3	4	3	3
Sines	3	3	3	1	3	3	3	4	4	4	4	3	3	1	3	4	4	4	3	4	4	4	4	4	4	4	3	4	-	3	1	3	4
Southampton	3	1	1	3	1	1	3	3	3	3	3	3	1	3	1	3	3	3	1	3	3	3	3	3	3	3	3	3	3	-	3	1	3
Tangier / Algericas	3	3	3	1	3	3	4	4	4	4	4	3	3	1	3	4	4	4	1	4	4	4	4	4	4	4	3	4	1	3	-	3	4
Thames Port / Tilbury	3	1	1	3	1	1	3	3	3	3	3	3	1	1	1	3	3	3	1	3	3	3	3	3	3	3	1	3	3	1	3	-	3
Veracruz	3	3	3	3	3	3	3	3	3	**2**	3	1	3	3	3	1	**2**	**2**	3	3	**2**	3	3	3	**2**	1	3	3	4	3	4	3	-

1 = fixed route; 2 = route calculated; 3 = route along transit point;
4 = same values as neighbouring harbour

To incorporate environmental influences on the duration, distance and fuel consumption of harbour to harbour voyages, weather scenarios had to be constructed. As it is very difficult to develop artificial weather scenarios, we decided to use weather data from sources as mentioned in the proceeding section. In order to refer to differences in fuel consumption, time and distance travelled, according to seasonal changes, a multitude of calculations for 30 time periods each in winter, spring, summer and fall for the year 2009 have been done.

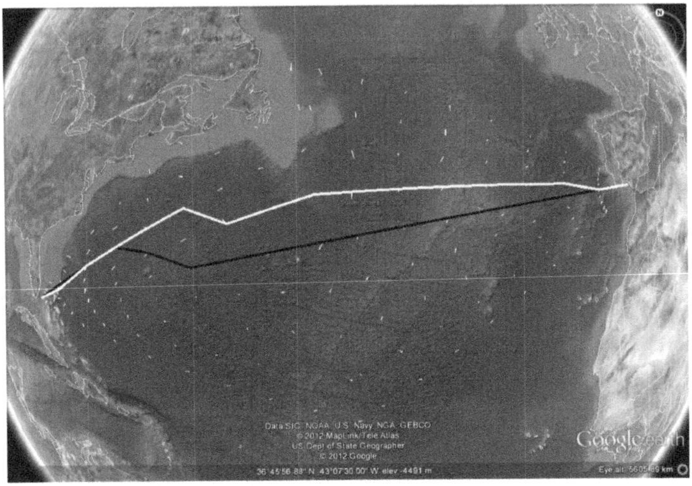

Figure 3.15: SPP from Cadiz to Miami, with (white) and without (black line) sail at 23 kn, displayed with Google Earth.

As an example the shortest path obtained from our modified label-setting algorithm between the harbours Cadiz and Miami for the 4,100 TEU ship 'Rafaela' with sail assisted propulsion is displayed as a white line and when travelling without a kite as a black line in Figure 3.15. When sailing at an average speed of 23 kn (selectable speed for each arc is 22 kn, 23 kn or 24 kn) the travel time sums up to 170 hours for 3,733nm with 408 tons of fuel consumed, when using sail assistance. When travelling without a sail, the same ship will only need 153 hours on 3,368nm but will consume 437 tons of fuel. This is a reduction in fuel consumption of 6.6%.

If this shortest path routing is used for an operational environmental routing with forecasted data for ships leaving the harbour at that specific moment, a higher resolution is advisable. This would of course lead to longer computing times, but the problem still could be solved within a reasonable time. If this routing algorithm is used, it could be enhanced to consider stochastic data which could better reflect the nature of weather data.

The regular SPP algorithm can be used for different objectives. The most obvious objective of course is finding the shortest path of a point to point relation. Another objective can be finding the path with minimum travel time. This modification of the SPP will be abbreviated MTTP (Minimum Travel Time Problem) in the following. Another modification of the SPP by changing the objective function is finding the path with the least fuel consumed which is abbreviated LFCP (Least Fuel Consumption Problem) in the following. Since we assume only one constant speed setting for all arcs of a network when using the SPP or one of its variations (LFCP or MTTP) the SPP and the MTTP will always provide the same path through the network with the same distance travelled, same amount of fuel consumed and same travel time needed. Therefore we will only refer to the results of the SPP for both objectives, minimum time and shortest path.

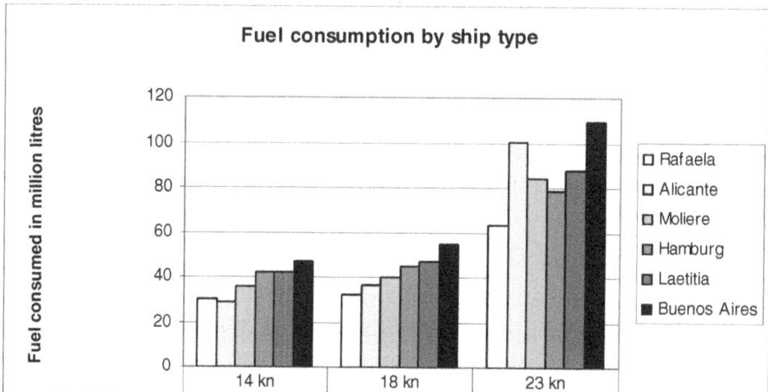

	14 kn	18 kn	23 kn
Rafaela	30,434,569	32,534,056	63,173,761
Alicante	28,504,145	36,352,580	100,147,351
Moliere	35,510,043	39,739,917	83,997,259
Hamburg	41,793,029	44,849,139	78,808,173
Laetitia	42,282,458	47,063,937	87,548,635
Buenos Aires	46,949,999	54,963,818	109,303,984

Figure 3.16: Fuel consumption by ship type

As shown in Figure 3.16, all ship types have increasing fuel consumption with increasing speed. For the average speed setting of 18 knots, fuel consumption also rises with the increasing size of the ships. This is also the case for an average speed setting of 14 knots, with the exception of ship Alicante, which consumes less than the smaller ship Rafaela at that speed setting. At an average speed setting of 23 knots these statements are not valid. Alicante as the second smallest ship has the second highest fuel consumption. Ship Moliere also has a higher consumption of fuel in regard to the next bigger ship Hamburg. The total amount of fuel consumed for all harbour connections the SPPTW algorithm was applied to (all connections marked 2 in Tabel 3.4) is higher for ship Alicante than the next three bigger ships, due to the fact that its maximal allowed service speed of 23.2 knots is almost reached with the average speed setting of 23 knots. The relatively low maximum service speed of 24.1 knots of ship Buenos Aires might as well be the reason for its extraordinary high fuel consumption in regard to the next smaller ship. All other ships have a maximum service speed above 25 knots (see Table 3.6).

Ship name	Rafaela	Alicante	Moliere	Hamburg	Laetitia	Buenos Aires
Maximum service speed in knots	25.4	23.2	25.6	25.6	25.3	24.1

Table 3.5: Ships maximum service speeds

Next, we will investigate the influence of the weather season on the fuel consumed for all connections considered in our test set. We compare the sum of fuel consumed, the travelled distance and travel time for four different main shipping routes. Harbour to harbour connections of two different regions were selected from the set of all harbour to harbour relations. These two regions are the North Atlantic and the Gulf of Mexico. Shipping routes crossing the North Atlantic were again divided into two sub sets, those where ships travel from the East to the West and those in the opposite direction from the West to the East. Again two subsets were generated for shipping routes in the Gulf of Mexico, with routes where ships travel from the North to the South and routes in the opposite direction from the South to the North. All ships, irrespectively of travelling with or without a sail assistance, show similar fuel consumption, travelled distance and travel time in regard to season and heading. Therefore, all characteristics can be shown by one example, which is the ship Laetitia in the following.

As shown in the Figure 3.17 and as already mentioned, fuel consumption rises exponential with an increase in speed. Figure 3.17 shows the total sum of fuel consumed for all harbour connections across the Atlantic Ocean in regard to direction of heading, season and speed for ship of type Laetita and is calculated as follows:

$$FC_{EW} = \sum_i \sum_j FC_{ij} \qquad \forall i \in H_{EA}; j \in H_{WA} \tag{3.25}$$

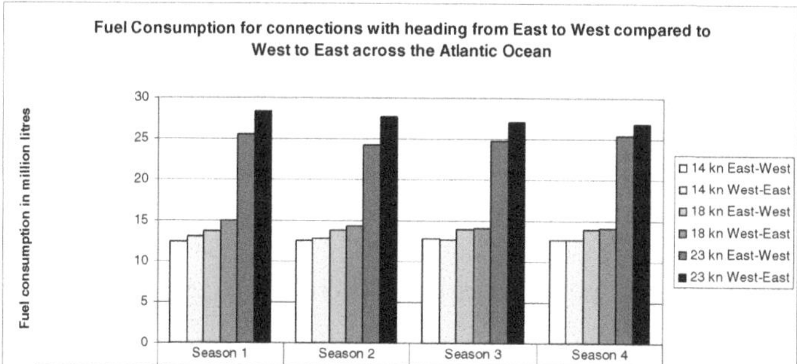

	Season 1	Season 2	Season 3	Season 4
14 kn East-West	12,396,963	12,556,357	12,732,916	12,659,626
14 kn West-East	13,078,893	12,799,720	12,673,161	12,587,168
18 kn East-West	13,680,802	13,766,183	13,891,885	13,940,912
18 kn West-East	14,958,680	14,303,887	14,049,670	14,091,346
23 kn East-West	25,503,559	24,302,976	24,783,913	25,457,396
23 kn West-East	28,398,916	27,748,381	27,066,040	26,849,788

Figure 3.17: Fuel consumption for travelling across the Atlantic Ocean without sail assistance on ship of type Laetitia.

$$FC_{WE} = \sum_i \sum_j FC_{ji} \qquad \forall i \in H_{EA}; j \in H_{WA} \qquad (3.26)$$

The total fuel consumption FC_{EW} for all harbour connections connecting harbours in the East Atlantic H_{EA} with those in the West Atlantic H_{WA} is the sum of all corresponding fuel consumed FC_{ij} between these harbours. The same is true for the West to East direction with the sum F_{WE} of fuel consumed on all connections between the harbours in the West Atlantic and those in the East Atlantic. As can be seen for all types of ships, fuel consumption is highest for season 1 and slightly decreasing from season to season on all shipping routes from the West to the East at 23 kn, with lowest values in season 4. For lower average speed settings of 14 and 18 knots, differences in fuel consumption for opposite headings is not as significant as it is for the 23 knots average speed setting. Differences are highest in season 1 (11.4% 23 kn, 9.3% 18 kn and 5.5% 14 kn) and drop down to almost zero (5.5% 23 kn 1.0% 18 kn and 0.6% 14 kn) in season 4.

Looking at the travelled distances for the same shipping routes reveals great differences for seasons but less differences in fuel consumption (see Figures 3.17 and 3.18). Season 1 with a great difference in fuel consumption on the other hand has the smallest differences in travelled distance (0,5% 14 kn, 0.1% 18 kn, 0.2% 23 kn) whereas for season 4 differences in travelled distance are highest (2.1% 14 kn, 2.5% 18 kn, 2.5% 23 kn). Only for speed settings of 14 and 18 knots in season 1, higher fuel consumption corresponds to longer travelled distances. In all other cases ships travel a little longer distances at a reduced fuel consumption. The reason for this might be that weather conditions and ocean currents allows for reduction in fuel consumption by manoeuvring longer distances on routes from East to West. In the opposite direction, no matter which route a ship takes, the weather and currents make it imposible to manoeuvre around obstructive weather conditions and so the optimal route reduces itself to the shortest path. Travel time was limited due to a given latest time of arrival and therefore as expected, it varies only slightly.

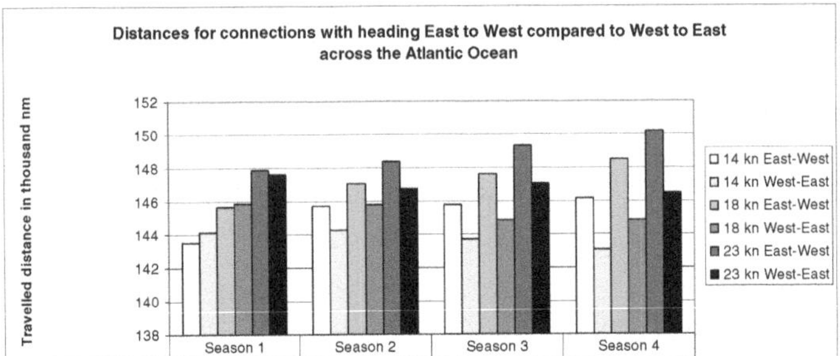

	Season 1	Season 2	Season 3	Season 4
14 kn East-West	143,510	145,709	145,797	146,156
14 kn West-East	144,164	144,279	143,688	143,088
18 kn East-West	145,654	147,059	147,589	148,500
18 kn West-East	145,837	145,758	144,834	144,834
23 kn East-West	147,829	148,389	149,273	150,185
23 kn West-East	147,587	146,719	147,071	146,479

Figure 3.18: Travelled distances for travelling across the Atlantic Ocean without sail assistance on ship of type Laetitia.

One might argue that fuel consumed in the Northern Atlantic for a route from the West to the East should be less than fuel consumed from the East to the West, due to winds blowing predominantly from the West. As wind is only one of the three influences we consider besides waves and ocean currents, this assumption might lead to wrong conclusions. Even waves that are coming from the rear, the same direction wind might blow from, has a braking effect on ships and might therefore compensate for pushing winds. In addition to that, the direction and force of ocean currents is in most cases totally independent from winds and waves direction and force.

When looking at the Gulf of Mexico, fuel consumption also changes according to the heading of the ship's routes (see Figure 3.19). Again for the example of the ship Laetitia representing all other types of ships, the fuel consumption varies most for the highest average speed setting of 23 knots (13.4% season 1; 1.6% season 2, 5.1% season 3, 8.0% season 4). The differences for the average speed setting of 18 knots are lowest with 1.0% for season 1, 6.5% for season 2, 0.0% for season 3 and 1.0% for season 4. For 14 knots average speed setting, differences are again higher (0.8% Season 1; 21.8% season 2, 17.3% season 3, 18.9% season 4). Differences in travelled distance and travel time are small (below 6% and below 6.5% respectively) (see Figure 3.19).

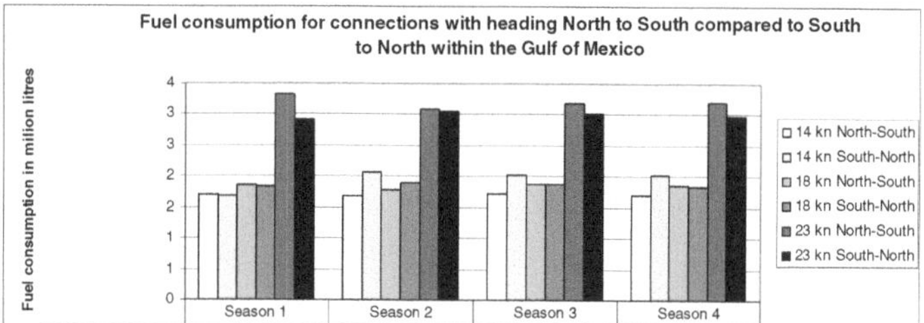

	Season 1	Season 2	Season 3	Season 4
14 kn North-South	1,694,816	1,688,587	1,728,784	1,708,159
14 kn South-North	1,681,363	2,058,298	2,027,321	2,031,182
18 kn North-South	1,848,017	1,778,640	1,867,466	1,860,982
18 kn South-North	1,829,728	1,895,004	1,867,090	1,841,883
23 kn North-South	3,322,605	3,088,306	3,171,392	3,203,101
23 kn South-North	2,917,765	3,036,761	3,016,328	2,966,184

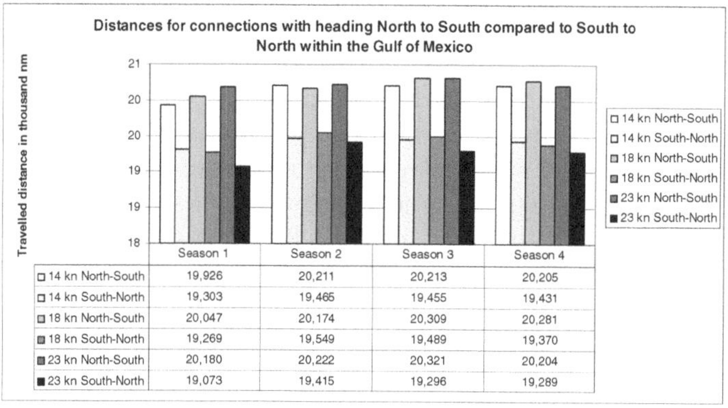

	Season 1	Season 2	Season 3	Season 4
14 kn North-South	19,926	20,211	20,213	20,205
14 kn South-North	19,303	19,465	19,455	19,431
18 kn North-South	20,047	20,174	20,309	20,281
18 kn South-North	19,269	19,549	19,489	19,370
23 kn North-South	20,180	20,222	20,321	20,204
23 kn South-North	19,073	19,415	19,296	19,289

Figure 3.19: Fuel consumption and travelled distances for travelling within the Gulf of Mexico.

When using sail assistance, all ship types can save fuel. Figure 3.20 shows the fuel savings, for all considered ship types, when using a sail assistance compared to the same ship type travelling without a sail assistance. The size of the kite used for these calculations is 160 m^2. Larger kites can produce a higher propulsion force and therefore lead to higher reductions in fuel consumption. The values in Figure 3.20 represent the mean fuel savings in percent and where obtained by calculating the shortest routes regarding

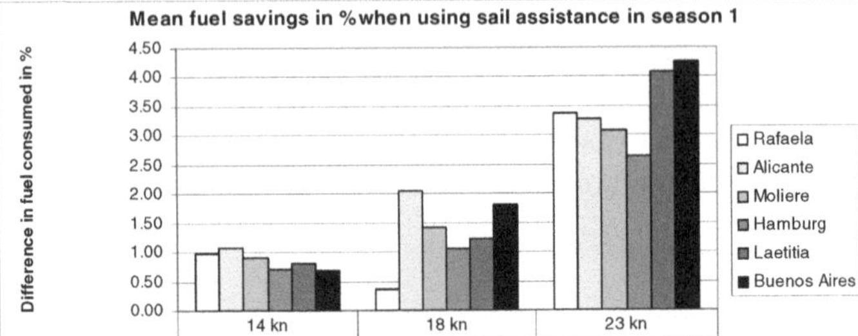

	14 kn	18 kn	23 kn
Rafaela	0.98	0.36	3.37
Alicante	1.08	2.05	3.27
Moliere	0.91	1.43	3.07
Hamburg	0.70	1.04	2.63
Laetitia	0.82	1.21	4.09
Buenos Aires	0.68	1.81	4.26

Figure 3.20: Mean fuel savings in % when using sail assistance.

minimal fuel consumption with the above introduced SPPTW algorithm for all harbour connections to which this algorithm could have been applied (marked with number 2 in Table 3.4). As the level of the savings is very similar for all seasons of the year, the results obtained are presented for season 1, representing all other seasons. For all ship types, the savings of fuel when using a sail assistance increases with higher speed settings. Only ship type Rafaela saves more fuel at the lower speed setting of 14 knots compared to the speed setting of 18 knots. The arrangement of ships in Figure 3.20 is according to their container carrying capacity sorted by increasing capacity from ship type Rafaela to ship type Buenos Aires as shown in Figure 3.21 .

At a lower speed setting, larger ships save less fuel than smaller ships. With an increase in speed this changes. At 23 knots average speed setting, the ratio of size to installed power might also have an impact on the amount of fuel saved. Ships with a powerful engine installed in relation to it container carrying capacity like the ship type Hamburg save less fuel in percent compared to a ship like Buenos Aires with a relatively small engine in relation to its container carrying capacity. But as explained in Section 3.4 the amount of parameters influencing the fuel consumption of a ship is high and therefore it is very difficult to assess the reasons for those different savings and therefore it is also difficult to determine the optimal configuration of a ship in order to save as much fuel as possible. This subject is addressed by optimal ship design. A short review on models and algorithms for defining the optimal ship design can be found in Christiansen et al. (2007, p. 202 - 205). For the above mentioned types of ships and considered speed settings,

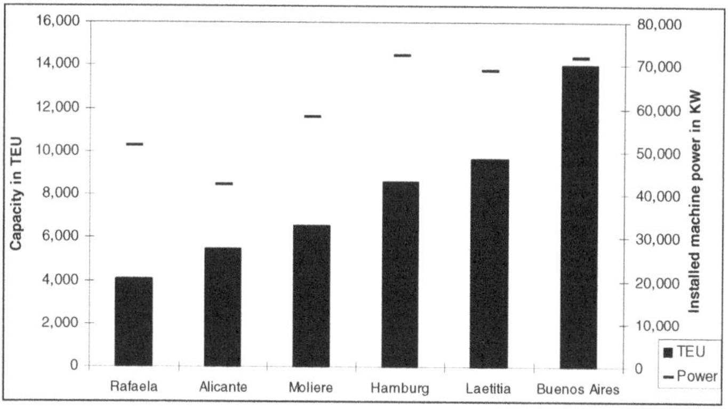

Figure 3.21: Carrying capacity in TEU and installed machine power for all ship types.

savings of fuel consumption are below 5% with rising fuel savings in regard to an increase in average speed setting.

Significant savings in fuel consumption can be found when comparing the SPPTW algorithm as introduced in Section 3.3 and the LFCP algorithm (see Figure 3.22). Again, all ships, no matter whether travelling with or without a sail assistance, show very similar results. Hence, results found when using ship Buenos Aires serve as an example.

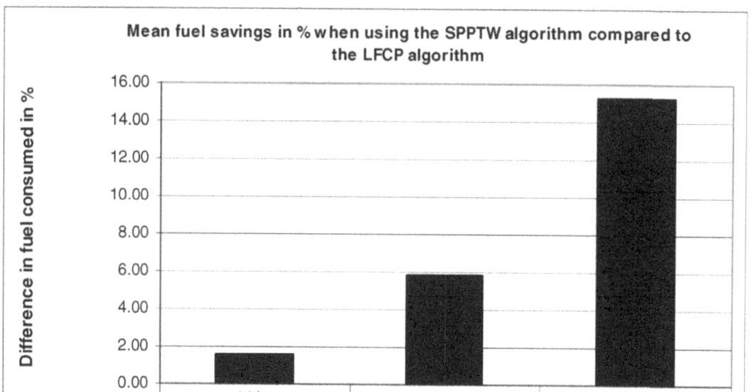

	14 kn	18 kn	23 kn
Hamburg(Sail)	1.58	5.88	15.30

Figure 3.22: Mean fuel savings in % when using the SPPTW algorithm compared to the LFCP algorithm.

Especially for average speed settings of 18 and 23 knots, savings are high. The reason for this might be that the SPPTW algorithm allows for a deviating speed of ± 1 kn to the given average speed settings. The LFCP algorithm only allows for one speed setting for the whole trip. In addition to just circumnavigating unfavourable weather conditions at a constant speed, ships can also travel slower at the beginning in order to wait for better weather conditions and can speed up afterwards to still maintain the expected latest time of arrival at the destination harbour. This additional degree of freedom in combination with the exponential rise in fuel consumption in accordance to rising speed, are most likely the reasons for the observed fuel savings. Other than the percentage of fuel saved, the savings of travelled distance and travel time are relatively small (ranging between 1% and 4% for all ship types) (see Figure 3.23). The reason for this might be that both algorithms navigate around unfavourable weather conditions, so that the path might be very similar, but only when a ship passes a specific network point, the route might change. Savings in travel time will almost always go along with an increase in fuel consumption due to a needed higher speed.

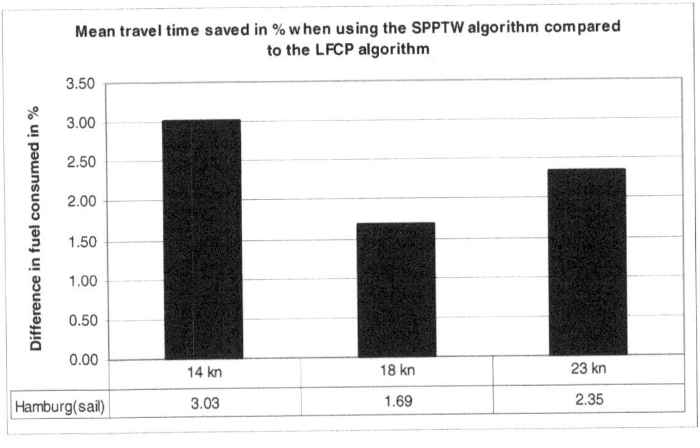

Figure 3.23: Mean travel time saved in % when using the SPPTW algorithm compared to the LFCP algorithm.

When comparing the results obtained from the SPPTW algorithm with the regular SPP algorithm, the percentage of fuel saved is even higher (see Figure 3.24). The SPP algorithm always finds slightly shorter distances as shown in Figure 3.25 but at an already mentioned higher fuel consumption. When using a shortest path route, ships will not navigate around unfavourable weather conditions.

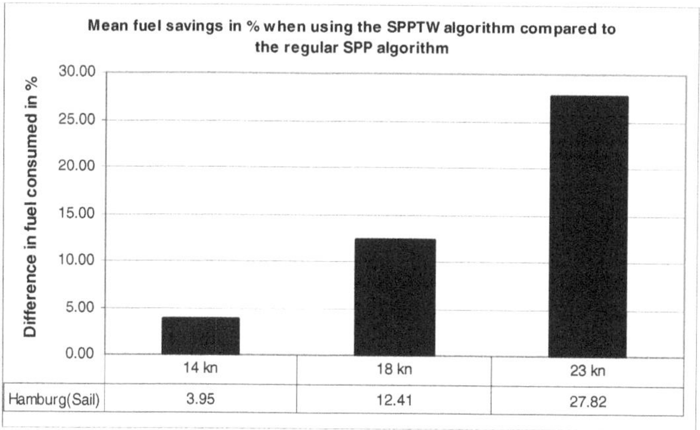

Figure 3.24: Mean fuel savings in % when using the SPPTW algorithm compared to the regular SPP algorithm.

When looking at the savings in mean travelled time (Figure 3.25) a reduction for speed settings of 18 and 23 knots (both 6.6% and 6.8%) is noticable. Only for the super slow speed setting of 14 knots, the travelled time is even higher (3.55%) than that received from the SPPTW algorithm. This again is due to the fact that the SPPTW algorithm allows for slightly slower and faster speed settings of ± 1 kn.

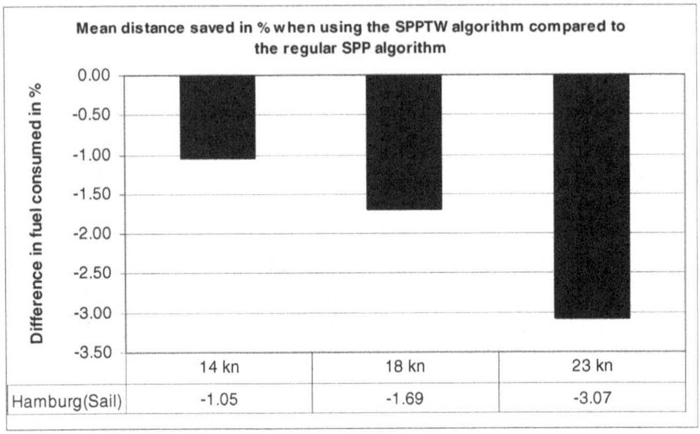

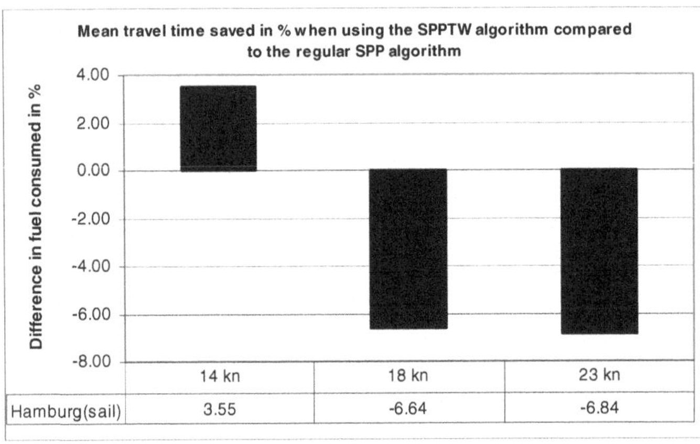

Figure 3.25: Mean distance and travel time saved in % when using the SPPTW algorithm compared to the regular SPP algorithm.

In all cases we were able to show that using a weather dependent Shortest Path Algorithm, with the objective to find the minimal fuel path, leads to dominating results in terms of saving fuel, compared to a regular SPP algorithm, which just minimises the travelled distance. When using the SPPTW algorithm, that even allows for slightly varying speed along a ships route from one to another harbour, savings in fuel are outstanding at least for a high average speed setting. We were also able to show that the seasons of the year have an influence on the amount of fuel consumed and the travelled distance, again for high average speed settings. Even though not very great, ships with an installed sail system consumed less fuel compared to the same type of ship with no sail system installed.

Chapter 4

Strategic Liner Network Design

In this chapter the reader is introduced to the main issue of this thesis: The liner shipping network design which determines the number of ships needed of a specific type to perform round trips and transporting as many cargo as profitable under the assumption of a given fleet of ships. The liner shipping network design is classified according to Christiansen et al. (2007) as a strategic planning task. The reader is introduced to liner shipping problems by a literature review in Section 4.1. In Section 4.2.2 we present a new Mixed Integer Programming model (MIP-model). Due to the complexity of the MIP-model and its resulting high computational time when solving larger test sets, a hybrid algorithm is presented in Section 4.3 which consists of a relaxed MIP-model and a Variable Neighbourhood Search (VNS). This hybrid algorithm solves larger test sets in far less computational time.

4.1 Literature

As already mentioned in Section 2.4, little research has been done on ship routing and scheduling and especially few contributions on the liner shipping network design can be found. A recent classification approach and literature review on liner shipping problems is given by Kjeldsen (2009).

Several research contributions on fleet design and ship routing make use of a predefined set of routes from which the most promising routes are selected via a set partitioning problem, as done in Fagerholt (1999, 2004) and Cho (1996). Fagerholt (1999) formulates the liner shipping task as a multi-trip vehicle routing problem, where cargoes are picked up in harbours next to a production facility and dropped off at harbours with a central depot. The size of a heterogeneous fleet of vessels is then determined.

Based on a multi-Travelling Salesman Problem with Time Windows,

Fagerholt et al. (2009) solves a fleet deployment problem in a liner shipping environment for a Ro-Ro vehicle transportation service. With a multi-start local search heuristic they are able to improve the planning results by 2 - 10% compared to manual planning solutions.

A proposal on how to design a strategic container liner shipping network and simultaneously solve an empty container redistribution planning problem is given by Shintani et al. (2007). They use a genetic algorithm-based heuristic to solve their two stage model. In difference to our model, empty space on ships is used to transport empty containers, for which a demand for each of the harbours considered is assumed. Only one ship is regarded, which has to visit each harbour at least once on the round trip. Instead of allowing for varying speeds on legs connecting two harbours an average speed is obtained, correlating with the requested weekly visiting frequency.

Examples of designing a feeder system for short sea operations is given in Bendall and Stent (2001) and Sigurd et al. (2005). The presented models generate optimal schedules in a hub & spoke network for ships operating from a hub and picking up cargo at several spoke-harbours. In the resulting schedule each harbour is visited only once in each round trip. To ensure the desired frequency of harbour visits, the necessary number of ships is determined. Ships operate at an assumed average speed. These pick up and delivery problems have a depot (hub) where all cargo is unloaded from all pick up harbours and cargo is loaded for all delivery harbours.

A mathematical model allowing for transhipment and multiple visits of a harbour in each round trip is presented by Agarwal and Ergun (2008). A round trip is assumed and speed variation is not a choice but given as a constant average setting. Three algorithms for this simultaneous ship-scheduling and cargo-routing problem are given: a greedy heuristic, Column Generation and Benders decomposition. These are compared with regard to computational efficiency and solution quality.

A recent study by Kjeldsen (2009), on how to design a liner shipping network is very similar to our described problem. As in our problem, Kjeldsen incorporates costs arising from speed dependent fuel consumption as the main issue of the objective function. Even though she takes transhipment and corresponding costs into account, her approach is based on a VRP that does not allow for ships to visit a harbour twice on a single round trip. Visiting a harbour on the inbound and outbound direction of a tour, is a special characteristic found in liner shipping routes in reality and has to be accounted for in liner shipping network design. In our approach, speed is a variable for each harbour to harbour relation. This is not the case for the problem described by Kjeldsen (2009). Here, the speed of a ship is set to an average speed for the complete round trip. In Kjeldsen (2009) the average speed for the complete round trip varies in integer speed steps between the lowest and the highest speed a ship can travel at for a longer time period.

The idea to model a liner shipping network problem with a vessel being able to stop at a harbour on its inbound and outbound journey, was first introduced by Rana and Vickson (1991). The task of this model is to find round trips for different type of ships, where cargo has to be loaded at its loading harbour and has to be unloaded at its destination harbours. This is modelled as a pick-up and delivery problem, where not all harbours regarded have to be visited. The starting as well as the ending harbour can be different for different types of ships. Additionally, the harbours where a ship starts and where it reverses the direction (beginning of the outbound journey), are not given in advance and therefore have to be determined by the model. A special characteristic of this model compared to other vehicle routing problems is that any node or harbour of the underlying network can be visited up to two times, once on the inbound part of a round trip and once on the outbound part. Rana and Vickson (1991) use a lagrangian relaxation approach to solve their non linear model, which is presented explicitly in the following:

Sets and Indices

$k \in K$	Set of ship types
$i, j, e, s \in H$	Set of harbours

Data

rev_{ij}	Revenue obtained from transporting a container from its origin i to its destination harbour j
c_{ijk}	Costs of a ship of type k for travelling from harbour i to harbour j
cap_{ijk}	Capacity of a ship of type k when travelling from harbour i to harbour j
$demand_{ij}$	Expected amount of container available for transportation from their origin harbour i to destination harbour j
t_k	Availability of a ship of type k measured in days
tl_{ik}	Required loading and unloading time of a ship of type k in harbour i
tt_{ijk}	Travel time, a ship of type k needs to travel from harbour i to harbour j
m	Sufficiently large number, for example $\max cap_{ijk}$

Variables

X_{ijk}	1, if harbour j is visited after harbour i on the round trip of a ship of type k; 0, otherwise
Y_{ijk}	Number of cargo loaded in TEU by a ship of type k from an origin harbour i to a destination harbour j
N_k	Number of round trips a ship of type k makes on its assigned route during one planning interval
D_{sek}	1, if s and e are turning point harbours for ship of type k; 0, otherwise

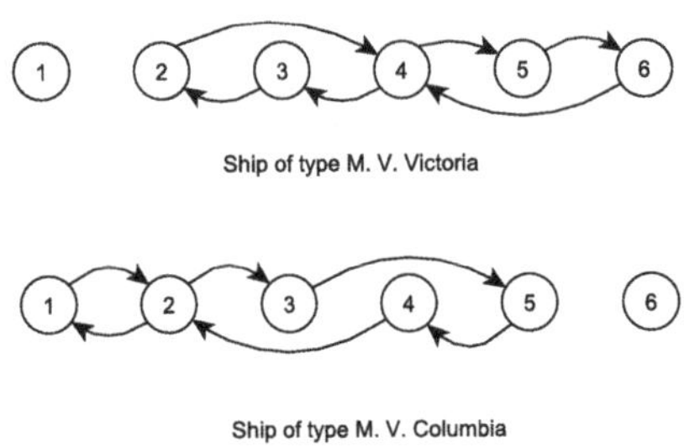

Figure 4.1: Example of harbour call sequences according to (Rana and Vickson 1991, p. 203)

As can be seen from Figure 4.1 ship of type M. V. Victoria has harbours 2 and 6 as turning point harbours. Variable D_{sek} therefore has value 1 for indices k = 'M. V. Victoria', $s = 2$ and $e = 6$. For ship of type k = 'M. V. Columbia' Variable D_{sek} has value 1 with turning point harbours $s = 1$ and $e = 5$. Decision variable X_{ijk} has value 1 for the example of ship of type k = 'M. V. Columbia' between harbours $i = 1$ and $j = 2$ or on the inbound part of the ships trip between harbours $i = 4$ and $j = 2$.

$$max : \sum_k \sum_i \sum_j N_k \cdot (rev_{ij} \cdot Y_{ijk} - c_{ijk} \cdot X_{ijk}) \tag{4.1}$$

The objective function maximizes the profit of transporting cargo from its origin to its destination harbour on a ship of type k on a ship type dependent round trip. The profit is obtained by subtracting all ship dependent travel costs from cargo dependent gained revenue. The capacity constraints (4.2) and (4.3) guarantee that a ship's capacity is not exceeded on any part of the round trip. These capacity constraints have been formulated for the outbound (4.2) and the inbound part of the round trip (4.3). The next four constraints (4.4) - (4.7) ensure that whenever a binary variables X_{ijk} or X_{jik} are zero for a specific harbour i, cargo can not be loaded or unloaded in this harbour. These constraints are again formulated for the inbound and outbound section of a ship's round trip and have been stated for a departure case (4.4) - (4.5) as well for the arrival case (4.6) - (4.7). The total amount of containers transported on all ships can not exceed the available demand, which is formulated in constraints (4.7).

$$\sum_{p=1}^{i} \sum_{q=j}^{|H|} Y_{pqk} \leq cap_{ijk} + M \cdot (1 - X_{ijk}) \quad \forall i,j,k | i < |H| \wedge j > i \tag{4.2}$$

$$\sum_{p=i}^{|} H| \sum_{q=1}^{j} Y_{pqk} \leq cap_{ijk} + M \cdot (1 - X_{ijk}) \quad \forall i,j,k | i > 2 \wedge j < i, \tag{4.3}$$

$$Y_{ijk} \leq \frac{demand_{ij}}{N_k} \sum_{p=i+1}^{J} X_{ipk} \quad \forall i,j,k | i < |H| \wedge j > i \tag{4.4}$$

$$Y_{ijk} \leq \frac{demand_{ij}}{N_k} \sum_{p=j}^{i-1} X_{ipk} \quad \forall i,j,k | i > 2 \wedge j < i \tag{4.5}$$

$$Y_{ijk} \leq \frac{demand_{ij}}{N_k} \sum_{p=i}^{j-1} X_{pjk} \quad \forall i,j,k | i < |H| \wedge j > i \tag{4.6}$$

$$Y_{ijk} \leq \frac{demand_{ij}}{N_k} \sum_{p=j+1}^{i} X_{pjk} \quad \forall i,j,k | i > 2 \wedge j < i \tag{4.7}$$

$$\sum_{k} N_k \cdot Y_{ijk} \leq demand_{ij} \quad \forall i,j | i \neq j \tag{4.8}$$

The network flow conservation is given in constraints (4.9)-(4.12). The newly introduced binary decision variable D_{sek} denotes the two turning point harbours s and e for each ship of type k. Constraints (4.9) and (4.10) assure that the turning point harbour s has to be left, for the outbound part of the trip and has to be called at, on the inbound part of the round trip respectively. Constraints (4.11) and (4.12) are classic flow conservation constraints, that guarantee that whenever a harbour p is visited on a round trip of a ship of type k, that harbour which lays either on the inbound or outbound part of the round trip between the turning point harbour s and e has to be left again. There is only one pair of turning point harbours for each ship type, as stated in constraints (4.13).

$$D_{sek} \cdot \left(\sum_{j=s+1}^{e} X_{sjk} - 1 \right) = 0 \qquad \forall s, e, k | s < H \wedge e > s \qquad (4.9)$$

$$D_{sek} \cdot \left(\sum_{j=s+1}^{e} X_{jsk} - 1 \right) = 0 \qquad \forall s, e, k | s < H \wedge e > s \qquad (4.10)$$

$$D_{sek} \cdot \left(\sum_{i=s}^{p-1} X_{ipk} - \sum_{j=p+1}^{e} X_{pjk} \right) = 0 \qquad \forall s, e, p, k$$

$$| s < H \wedge e > s \wedge s < p < e \qquad (4.11)$$

$$D_{sek} \cdot \left(\sum_{i=p+1}^{e} X_{ipk} - \sum_{j=s}^{p-1} X_{pjk} \right) = 0 \qquad \forall s, e, p, k$$

$$| s < H \wedge e > s \wedge s < p < e \qquad (4.12)$$

$$\sum_{s,e} D_{sek} \leq 1 \qquad \forall k \qquad (4.13)$$

The sum of all travel and loading times of each ship shall not exceed the planing interval (see constraints (4.14)). Within one planning interval a ship can make multiple round trips which is denoted by variable N_k.

$$\sum_i tl_{ik} \sum_j X_{ijk} + \sum_i \sum_j tt_{ijk} \cdot X_{ijk} \leq \frac{t_k}{N_k} \qquad \forall k \qquad (4.14)$$

Except for the ship independent cargo constraints, that remain part of the master problem, all other constraints are solved individually for each ship type in subproblems. With this lagrangean relaxation and its decomposition, the nonlinearity of the cargo constraints is transferred into the mixed integer restricted master problem. The nonlinearity in the subproblem constraints still remain, if each subproblem represents one ship type. To compensate for this, Rana and Vickson (1991) further decomposed the network constraints (4.9)-(4.13). Binary variable D_{sek} is now eliminated and replaced by a set of turning point harbours s and e as given data. Hence, the restricted master problem only assures that cargo is efficiently transported on different ship type - round trip combinations.

According to the classification scheme presented by Kjeldsen (2009), our decision problem would be classified as shown in Table 4.4.

Nr.	Characteristics	Options	Classification
1	Number of intersection points	None	-
		One	-
		Multiple	But no transhipment
2	Type of Operation	Delivery	-
		Pick-up	-
		Pick-up and delivery separated	-
		Pick-up and delivery interwoven	X
3	Nature of demand	Deterministic	X
		Stochastic	-
		Dependent on service	-
4	Scheduling constraints at the harbour	Time of service fixed in advance	-
		Time windows	-
		No restrictions	(Un-)loading times given
5	Number of ships	Fixed	-
		Changeable - constant over scheduling period	X
		Changeable - changes over scheduling period	-
6	Fleet composition	Heterogeneous	Diff. capacity, costs, propulsion
		Homogeneous	-
7	Cruising speed	Yes	Per harbour to harbour relation
		No	-
8	Demand splitting	Allowed	-
		Not allowed	X
9	Partial satisfaction of demand	Allowed	X
		Not allowed	-
10	Number of commodities	One	Only TEU container
		Multiple	-
11	Cargo transhipment	Allowed	-
		Not allowed	X
12	Number of routes	One	-
		Multiple	For each type of ship one route
13	Planning interval	Defined - ships must finish routes	harbour visiting frequency dependent
		Defined - ships need not finish	-
		Undefined	-
14	Ships required to be empty	Yes	-
		No	X
15	Harbour precedence requirements	Exist	-
		None	X
16	Ship-harbour compatibility	Exist	(X)
		None	X
17	Cost types	Fixed costs	
		•in operation	X
		•in lay-up	X
		Variable costs	
		•steaming costs	X
		•harbour entry charges	(X)
		•time spend in harbour	(X)
		•cargo operation	(X)
		•transhipment	-
		•Cost of unserviced demand	-
18	Objective	Minimize costs	-
		Maximize profits	X
		Minimizing environmental impact	impact accounted for

For classifications marked (X) our new MIP model for the strategic network design can easily be expanded

Table 4.4: Classification scheme according to Kjeldsen (2009)

Intersection points, the first characteristic, describe where cargo can be transhipped, between two different liner services or where a ship has a depot. For most liner shipping problems a depot is not needed, since ships in a liner service operate non-stop around the clock. In some cases a depot is needed for modelling reasons. When modelling a depot, standard formulations similar to the VRP can be used. This way ships would have a depot as an intersection point from where different routes would start, as done in Kjeldsen (2009). In her case the routes add up to a combined liner service. In our modelling approach harbours can be visited by different liner services, but transhipment of cargo between these services is not possible. We believe that transhipment harbours of hub & spoke networks can be determined by a separate transhipment harbour location problem. Cargo that is transhipped in one or two transhipment harbours, will have the transhipment harbours as its pick-up and destination harbours in our routing problem. Thus, spokes in a hub & spoke environment are not considered. We do not yet have scheduling constraints at harbours but we account for a number of cargo dependent loading and unloading times. The fleet of ships is heterogeneous among all liner services. However, the fleet of ships is homogeneous within a single liner service. This is due to the assumption that cargo demand in the harbours stays at a weekly recurring average level and only ships with the same capacity can guarantee loading all assigned cargo. Ships of different liner services may differ in their capacity, cost structure and (additional) propulsion system. Our model assigns each type of ship a different liner service and the planning interval is undefined. The minimum length of a planning interval depends on the length of a liner service's round trip, the selected speed and the desired harbour visiting frequency. For the first time we will account for monthly mean weather dependent travel times and resulting travel costs, as well as variable speed settings on arcs between two consecutive harbours for a strategic liner network design problem.

4.2 Decision Problem and Mixed Integer Programming Model

4.2.1 Decision Problem

In the following we present a description of the decision problem and than a mathematical model formulation for a strategic liner network design problem. For each type of ship we create round trips that specify the harbours to be visited by this type of ship and its corresponding schedule. This is done for multiple types of ships simultaneously leading to round trips individually dedicated to each type of ship.

Our objective is to maximize the profit gained by revenues when transporting cargo from its pick-up harbour to its destination harbour and subtracting all variable speed and type of ship dependent travel costs as well as fixed charter costs per ship (see objective function (4.15)). Not all cargo demand has to be transported. Only cargo that contributes to maximizing profits will be serviced.

Our MIP-model will address the following questions:

- Which harbours on a ship's route should be visited on a liner round trip?
- Which cargo can be transported from the cargo's pick-up harbour to its destination harbour along the same round trip?
- How many ships of a specific type are needed to guarantee an e.g. weekly visit to all harbours along a round trip?
- Which average speed should be selected on a trip between two consecutive harbours? Or in other words, how long does it take to reach the next harbour in line?

In our notation each cargo $c \in C$ has a loading and a corresponding unloading harbour. Split deliveries are not allowed. A cargo c consists of multiple containers measured in TEU. Different cargoes with the same loading and unloading harbour may vary in size (amount of TEU), maximum allowed transportation time and achievable revenue. It is assumed that all cargo at each harbour emerges as a transportation demand based on a weekly average. Indices h, i, $j \in H$ indicate harbours, where all loading or unloading harbours can be visited on the inbound or outbound part of a round trip. We assume that the sequence of harbours that can be visited on a round trip is given. Not all harbours have to be visited, but the less harbours are visited, the less cargo can be transported and therefore less profit might be generated. If a harbour is visited on the inbound trip the direction indicator d, $e \in D$ has value 1 and for a visit on the outbound trip, value 2 (see Figure 4.5). Harbours in a liner shipping network are usually aligned along the shoreline like a chain of pearls (see also Figures 4.2-4.4).

We will not consider transhipment of cargoes. In contrast to the model described by Rana and Vickson (1991) we will have the following features:

- The ship's speed on a route between two harbours is selected
- Our model will be a linear (instead of a non linear) MIP-model

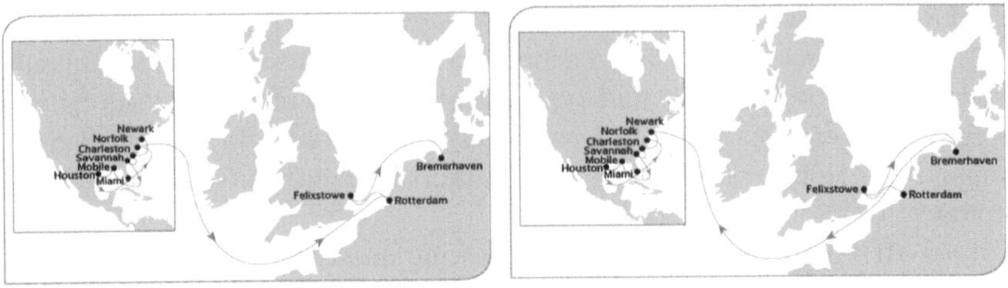

Figure 4.2: Maersk Transatlantic (TA2) – east- and westbound, Maersk (2011)

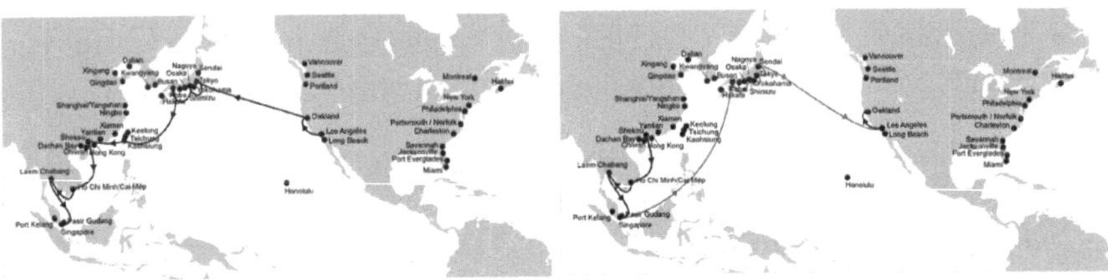

Figure 4.3: Hapag-Lloyd South China Sea Expr. (SCX) – east- and westbound, Hapag-Lloyd (2011)

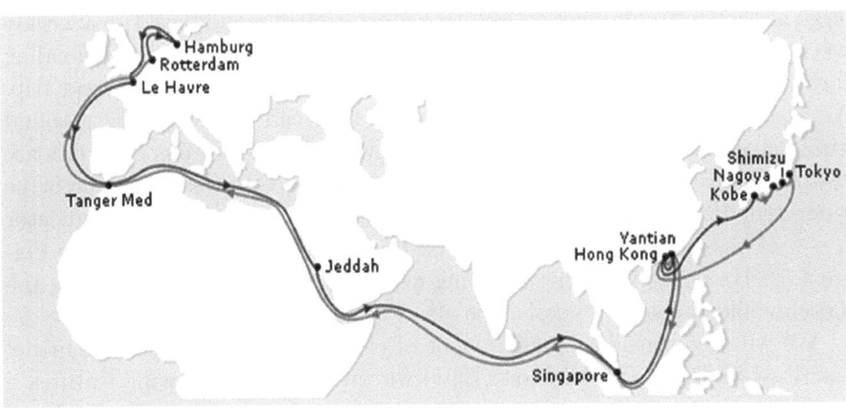

Figure 4.4: CMA CGM French Asia Line 12, CGM (2011)

- Different type of cargo and therefore different revenue contribution is accounted for

- Cargo has to be picked up and then delivered to its designated unloading harbour within a given time window

4.2.2 Mixed Integer Programming Model

In the model the harbours are numbered according to their geographical position, beginning with the most westward harbour with an index of 1 and ending with the most eastward harbour with an index as high as the total number of harbours.

Ships of type $k \in K$ represent ships of the same kind with identical capacity and cost structure. The average speed a vessel should select when travelling between two successive harbours is indicated by $v \in V$. The set of all cargoes $(c, d(i), d(j))$ that stay on board a ship of type k when passing harbour h in direction d) is expressed by the set $CargoRoute_{hdk}$. For example (see Figure 4.5) the load harbour of a cargo c is $i = 4$ and the unload harbour $j = 5$, harbours 2, 3 and 6 are those harbours (h, d) that may be passed by with cargo c on board the ship. All four potential routes for cargoes are generated in a pre-processing step. These are for our example: a) $d(4) = 1$, $d(5) = 1$; b) $d(4) = 1$, $d(5) = 2$; c) $d(4) = 2$, $d(5) = 1$ and d) $d(4) = 2$, $d(5) = 2$. Given the liner service shown in Figure 4.5 only alternative b) and d) will be used, where harbour 5 is visited on the outbound part of the round trip. As we will see later, alternatives c) and d) will not be chosen in such a setting because a cargo is forced to stay on board a ship as short as possible.

$Load_i$ describes the set of cargoes c that can be picked up in harbour i and $Unload_i$ indicates the set of all cargoes that can be unloaded in harbour i respectively.

$demand_c$ is the amount of cargo c in TEU, which arises every week. The revenue per TEU that can be obtained is given by rev_c. The time a ship of type k needs, when travelling from harbour i to j in direction d at a speed v is given with tt_{ijdkv}. $ttt^{max}_{i(c)d(i)j(c)d(j)k}$indicates how long a ship is allowed to transport cargo c from its loading $i(c)$ to its unloading harbour $j(c)$, which can either be on the inbound or outbound part of a round trip indicated by $d(i)$ and $d(j)$ for the loading and unloading harbour respectively. $costs_{ijkv}$ are the speed dependent variable travel costs for a ship of type k when travelling from harbour i to j directly. These are the costs we receive from our operational, shortest path problem under environmental influences. $charter_k$ are the daily charter-rates representing the fixed costs to operate a

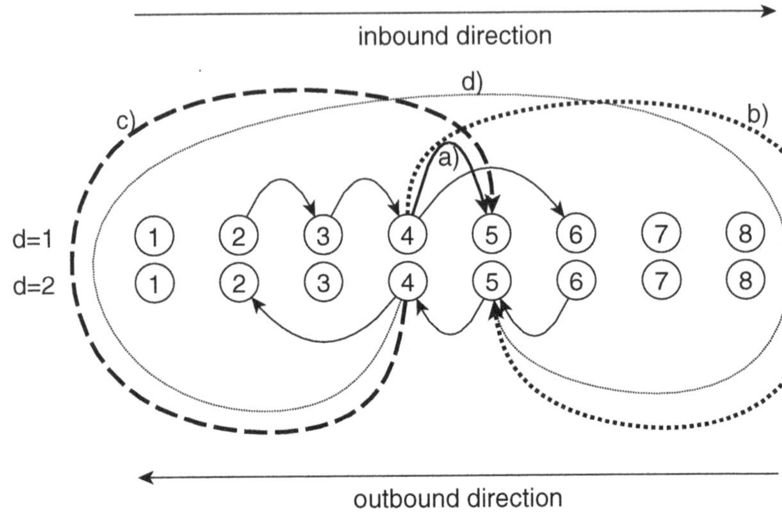

Figure 4.5: Possible routes of a cargo from load harbour $i = 4$ to unload harbour $j = 5$ on a ship's round trip.

ship of type k for one day, which include costs for personnel, amortization and other fixed charges. $tload_{ck}$and $tunload_{ck}$ are loading and unloading times of cargo c on board of a ship of type k, at their loading ($loadH_c$) and unloading harbours ($unloadH_c$).

Decision variables $Ship_k$ take value 1 if a ship of type k is in use, 0 otherwise. $NShips_k$ is the number of ships of type k that are needed to guarantee a weekly (every 168 h) visit for all visited harbours on the round trip. H_{idk} has value 1, if harbour i is visited by a ship of type k either on the inbound (d=1) or outbound (d=2) part of the round trip, 0 otherwise. The inbound part of the round trip is indicated by increasing harbour indices, whereas the harbours of the outbound part have indices in a decreasing order. TH_{ik}^W (TH_{jk}^E) is equal to 1, if harbour i (j respectively) is the most westerly (easterly) harbour of the round trip of a ship of type k. For the example shown in Figure 4.5 the most westerly turning point harbour is the harbour with index 2 and the most easterly turning point harbour is the harbour with index 6. X_{ijdk}has value 1, if a ship of type k is travelling directly from harbour i to harbour j in direction d, without stopping at harbours that lie in between. Inbound and outbound trips are viewed separately. Y_{cdk} has value 1, if cargo c is picked up on the inbound or outbound part d of the round trip of a ship of type k, 0 otherwise. Binary variables $Z_{cd(i)d(j)k}$ indicate, whether cargo c is picked up at its origin harbour i and dropped off at its destination harbour j on either the inbound or outbound trip $(d(i), d(j))$ of a ship of type k's round trip. $V_{i,j,d,k,v}$ has value 1, if a ship of type k is travelling with speed v from harbour i to harbour j in direction d.

The travel time of the direct connection between harbours i and j for a ship of type k's round trip is represented by the decision variable TT_{ijk}. $Hde_{(id)k}$ is the point in time when a ship of type k is leaving harbour i on the in- or outbound part of its round trip and $Har_{(id)k}$is the point in time when a ship of type k arrives at harbour i respectively.

The MIP-model can be formulated as follows:

$$max: \sum_c \sum_d \sum_k rev_c \cdot demand_c \cdot Y_{cdk} - \sum_i \sum_j \sum_d \sum_k \sum_v costs_{ijkv} \cdot V_{ijdkv} - \sum_k NShips_k \cdot charter_k \tag{4.15}$$

$$Y_{cdk} = \sum_{d(j)} Z_{cd(i)d(j)k} \qquad \forall c, d(i), k \tag{4.16}$$

$$\sum_k \sum_d Y_{cdk} \leq 1 \qquad \forall c \tag{4.17}$$

$$H_{Loadh(c)dk} \geq \sum_{d(j)} Z_{cd(i)d(j)k} \qquad \forall c, d(i), k \tag{4.18}$$

$$H_{Unloadh(c)dk} \geq \sum_{d(i)} Z_{cd(i)d(j)k} \qquad \forall c, d(j), k \tag{4.19}$$

$$\sum_{c \in LoadH_h} demand_c \cdot Y_{cdk} + \sum_c \sum_{(d(i),d(j)) \in CargoRoutes_{(hd)k}} demand_c \cdot Z_{cd(i)d(j)k} \leq cap_{hdk} \qquad \forall h, d, k \tag{4.20}$$

The objective function (4.15) maximizes the profit obtained by revenues from transporting cargo c on the round trip of a ship of type k and subtracting all speed dependent travel costs as well as fixed daily charter-rates per ship. Constraints (4.16) require that when loading cargo c, a feasible round trip containing the pick-up harbour of cargo c is taken. A cargo can be loaded on a ship only once, either on the inbound or outbound trip of a ship of type k, which is ensured by (4.17). If cargo c is loaded at its pick-up harbour by a ship of type k (constraints (4.18)) or unloaded at its destination harbour (constraints (4.19)), variable H_{idk} becomes 1. The capacity constraints (4.20) ensure that the capacity of a ship of type k is never exceeded, when leaving a harbour on any possible cargo route.

In general the following flow conservation constraints (4.21) - (4.30) denote that the tour a ship of type k makes, is one closed round trip without internal closed loops. Constraints (4.21) and (4.22) ensure that whenever harbour j is visited from a harbour with a smaller index, it has to be left again on an arc to a harbour with a greater index unless it is a turning point harbour. j can either be a harbour in between the turning point harbours of the round trip or a turning point harbour itself, as modelled in constraints (4.21). Due to constraints (4.22) - (4.24) it is guaranteed that a harbour is left again after it has been visited on either the inbound trip or outbound trip. Constraints (4.22) ensure that the harbour visiting variables H_{j1k} are 1, if harbour j is left on the inbound part of the ship's route. Constraints (4.23) and (4.24) ensure that variable H_{j2k} is 1 if a ship visits (4.23) or leaves (4.24) harbour j on its outbound trip.

Harbours with the smallest and highest index have to be viewed separately as they are not included in the previous flow conservation constraints. Constraints (4.25) and (4.26) ensure that whenever these outermost harbours are visited, they have to be left again in the other direction and therefore must be turning point harbours. There must be a turning point harbour on either side of the round trip, which is ensured by constraints (4.27) and (4.28). All harbours with a smaller (greater) index than the turning point harbour with the smallest (greatest) index, can not be visited (constraints (4.29) and (4.30)).

$$TH^W_{jk} + \sum_{i|i<j} X_{ij1k} = \sum_{i|i>j} X_{ji1k} + TH^E_{jk} \qquad \forall j,k \qquad (4.21)$$

$$TH^E_{jk} + \sum_{h|h>j} X_{jh1k} = H_{j1k} \qquad \forall j,k \mid j < |J| \qquad (4.22)$$

$$TH^E_{jk} + \sum_{i|i>j} X_{ij2k} = H_{j2k} \qquad \forall j,k \mid j < |J| \qquad (4.23)$$

$$TH^W_{jk} + \sum_{h|h<j} X_{jh2k} = H_{j2k} \qquad \forall j,k \qquad (4.24)$$

$$TH^W_{1k} \cdot 2 = H_{12k} + H_{11k} \qquad \forall k \qquad (4.25)$$

$$TH^E_{|I|k} \cdot 2 = H_{|I|2k} + H_{|I|1k} \qquad \forall k \qquad (4.26)$$

$$\sum_{j|j>1} TH^E_{jk} = Ship_k \qquad \forall k \qquad (4.27)$$

$$\sum_{j|j<|J|} TH^W_{jk} = Ship_k \qquad \forall k \qquad (4.28)$$

$$\sum_d H_{idk} \leq 2 - 2 \cdot TH^W_{jk} \qquad \forall i, j, k \mid i < j \qquad (4.29)$$

$$\sum_d H_{hdk} \leq 2 - 2 \cdot TH^E_{jk} \qquad \forall h, j, k \mid h > j \qquad (4.30)$$

Constraints (4.31) - (4.43) deal with arrival times of all visited harbours, speed selection between two consecutive harbours and the frequency with which each harbour is visited. Whenever a ship of type k is travelling from harbour i to j either on its inbound or outbound part of the round trip, constraints (4.31) ensure that variables V_{ijdks} have to be 1 for one of the possible average speed selections.

Constraints (4.32) verify that the harbour arrival time in the next, following harbour is the sum of the departure time of the previous harbour plus the average speed dependent travel time on the passage between two consecutive harbours.

Depending on the time needed for loading and unloading cargo at a specific harbour, the harbour arrival and departure times are calculated in constraints (4.33). It is unlikely that the combination of optimal speed selection between the harbours and the duration for loading and unloading cargo at all harbours will exactly add up to a multiple of the desired inverse of the frequency. Therefore a slack time at each visited harbour is added. This slack time $Slack_{idk}$ can either be a waiting time for ships that lie in the roads waiting until they can be unloaded at a harbour, or it can be used for smaller repairs and overhauls of the ship. Another possibility of interpreting this slack time is to view it as a safety time that might compensate for unpredictable circumstances and weather phenomena.

Constraints (4.34) guarantee that the arrival times at harbours on the outbound trip have to be larger than the departure time of all harbours visited on the inbound trip. The maximum total round trip time is set in constraints (4.35). The arrival time in the last harbour – being the harbour with the smallest index and therefore also the starting harbour – has to be smaller or equal to a multiple of the inverse of the desired frequency. To ensure this frequency, a specific amount of ships of the same type k are needed, as denoted in constraints (4.36).

The slack time in all visited harbours can not be greater than the time between two consecutive visits at the same harbour, which is just the inverse of the desired frequency (constraints (4.37)).

The following six constraints (4.38) to (4.43) ensure for all possible cargo route combinations that the allowed and predefined maximum total travel time of a cargo c is not exceeded. Those constraints are divided into various cases:

1. The pick-up harbour has a smaller index than the destination harbour with direction combinations $d(i)=1$, $d(j)=1$; or $d(i)=2$, $d(j)=2$.

2. Another case describes the same in- and outbound combinations but with the pick-up harbour of cargo c having a greater index than the index of the corresponding unload harbour (constraints (4.40) and (4.41)).

The other remaining cases (constraints (4.42) and (4.43)) represent the situation where the loading harbour of cargo c is on the opposite side of the round trip to the corresponding unloading harbour ($d(i)= 1$; $d(j)= 2$ and $d(i)= 2$; $d(j)= 1$). In this case it does not matter whether the loading harbour of cargo c has a smaller or greater index than its unloading harbour.

$$\sum_{v} V_{ijdkv} = X_{ijdk} \qquad \forall i,j,d,k|(i<j \wedge d=1) \vee (i>j \wedge d=2) \tag{4.31}$$

$$Hde_{i1k} + \sum_{v} tt_{ij1kv} \cdot V_{ij1kv} \leq Har_{j1k} \qquad \forall i,j,k|i<j \tag{4.32}$$

$$Hde_{i2k} + \sum_{v} tt_{ij2kv} \cdot V_{ij2kv} \leq Har_{j2k} \qquad \forall i,j,k|i>j \tag{4.33}$$

$$\begin{aligned} Hde_{jdk} + \sum_{c \in unloadH_c} \sum_{e} tunload_{ck} \cdot Z_{cedk} + \\ \sum_{c \in loadH_c} \sum_{e} tload_{ck} \cdot Z_{cedk} + Slack_{jdk} \leq Har_{jdk} \qquad \forall j,d,k \end{aligned} \tag{4.34}$$

$$Hde_{j1k} \leq Har_{j2k} \qquad \forall j,k \tag{4.35}$$

$$Har_{j2k} \leq \frac{1}{f} \cdot NShips_k \qquad \forall j,k \tag{4.36}$$

$$Slack_{idk} \leq \frac{1}{f} \cdot H_{idk} \qquad \forall i, d, k \tag{4.37}$$

$$\begin{aligned} &Har_{unloadH_c,1,k} - Hde_{loadH_c,1,k} \leq \\ &t_c^{max} + (ttt^{max}_{loadH_c,1,unloadH_c,1,k} - t_c^{max}) \\ &\cdot(1 - Z_{c,1,1,k}) \qquad \forall c, k | loadH_c < unloadH_c \wedge \\ &\qquad ttt^{max}_{loadH_c,1,unloadH_c,1,k} > t_c^{max} \end{aligned} \tag{4.38}$$

$$\begin{aligned} &\frac{1}{f} \cdot NShips_k - Hde_{loadH_c,2,k} \\ &-Har_{unloadH_c,2,k} \leq t_c^{max} + \\ &(ttt^{max}_{loadH_c,2,unloadH_c,2,k} - t_c^{max}) \\ &\cdot(1 - Z_{c22k}) \qquad \forall c, k | loadH_c < unloadH_c \wedge \\ &\qquad ttt^{max}_{loadH_c,2,unloadH_c,2,k} > t_c^{max} \end{aligned} \tag{4.39}$$

$$\begin{aligned} &Har_{unloadH_c,2,k} - Hde_{loadH_c,1,k} \leq \\ &t_c^{max} + (ttt^{max}_{loadH_c,1,unloadH_c,2,k} - t_c^{max}) \\ &\cdot(1 - Z_{c11k}) \qquad \forall c, k | \\ &\qquad ttt^{max}_{loadH_c,1,unloadH_c,2,k} > t_c^{max} \end{aligned} \tag{4.40}$$

$$\begin{aligned} &\frac{1}{f} \cdot NShips_k - Hde_{loadH_c,2,k} \\ &-Har_{unloadH_c,1,k} \leq t_c^{max} + \\ &(ttt^{max}_{loadH_c,2,unloadH_c,1,k} - t_c^{max}) \\ &\cdot(1 - Z_{c21k}) \qquad \forall c, k | \\ &\qquad ttt^{max}_{loadH_c,2,unloadH_c,1,k} > t_c^{max} \end{aligned} \tag{4.41}$$

$$\begin{aligned} &\frac{1}{f} \cdot NShips_k - Hde_{loadH_c,1,k} \\ &-Har_{unloadH_c,1,k} \leq t_c^{max} + \\ &(ttt^{max}_{loadH_c,1,unloadH_c,1,k} - t_c^{max}) \\ &\cdot(1 - Z_{c11k}) \qquad \forall c, k | loadH_c > unloadH_c \wedge \\ &\qquad ttt^{max}_{loadH_c,1,unloadH_c,1,k} > t_c^{max} \end{aligned} \tag{4.42}$$

$$Har_{unloadH_c,2,k} - Hde_{loadH_c,2,k} \leq t_c^{max} + (ttt^{max}_{loadH_c,2,unloadH_c,2,k} - t_c^{max}) \cdot (1 - Z_{c22k}) \quad \forall c,k | loadH_c > unloadH_c \wedge ttt^{max}_{loadH_c,2,unloadH_c,2,k} > t_c^{max} \tag{4.43}$$

Cuts constructed in constraints (4.44) to (4.47) reduce the solution space and thus reduce computational times. These ensure that a cargo is unloaded as early as possible and does not stay longer on board than necessary. In case the unloading harbour of a cargo c is visited on the inbound and outbound part of a ship's round trip, the cargo is unloaded as early as possible, which is the first time the unloading harbour of a cargo has been reached after pick-up. That way the cargo does not block the ship's capacity and other cargo can be loaded on-board.

The remaining constraints (4.48) to (4.55) and (4.56) to (4.59) define binary variables and non-negative variables respectively.

$$Z_{c12k} \leq 1 - H_{loadH_c,1,k} \quad \forall c,k | loadH_c \leq unloadH_c \wedge ttt^{max}_{loadH_c,1,unloadH_c,2,k} > t_c^{max} \tag{4.44}$$

$$Z_{c22k} \leq 1 - H_{loadH_c,1,k} \quad \forall c,k | loadH_c \leq unloadH_c \wedge ttt^{max}_{loadH_c,2,unloadH_c,2,k} > t_c^{max} \tag{4.45}$$

$$Z_{c21k} \leq 1 - H_{loadH_c,2,k} \quad \forall c,k | loadH_c \leq unloadH_c \wedge ttt^{max}_{loadH_c,2,unloadH_c,1,k} > t_c^{max} \tag{4.46}$$

$$Z_{c11k} \leq 1 - H_{loadH_c,2,k} \quad \forall c,k | loadH_c \leq unloadH_c \wedge ttt^{max}_{loadH_c,1,unloadH_c,1,k} > t_c^{max} \tag{4.47}$$

$$Ship_k \in \{0,1\} \quad \forall k \tag{4.48}$$

$$NShips_k \in \{0,1\} \quad \forall k \tag{4.49}$$

$$TH^{max}_{ik} \in \{0,1\} \quad \forall i,k \tag{4.50}$$

$$TH^{E}_{ik} \in \{0,1\} \quad \forall i,k \tag{4.51}$$

$$H_{idk} \in \{0,1\} \quad \forall i,d,k \tag{4.52}$$

$$X_{ijdk} \in \{0,1\} \quad \forall i,j,d,k \tag{4.53}$$

$$Y_{cdk} \in \{0,1\} \quad \forall c,d,k \tag{4.54}$$

$$Z_{cdek} \in \{0,1\} \quad \forall c,d,e,k \tag{4.55}$$

$$V_{ijdkv} \geq 0 \quad \forall i,j,d,k,v \tag{4.56}$$

$$Har_{idk} \geq 0 \quad \forall i,d,k \tag{4.57}$$

$$Hde_{idk} \geq 0 \qquad \forall i, d, k \qquad (4.58)$$
$$Slack_{idk} \geq 0 \qquad \forall i, d, k \qquad (4.59)$$

In principle the above MIP-model can be solved by a standard MIP solver. However, to solve models of realistic size, we have created a hybrid algorithm, consisting of a VNS and a relaxed MIP-model. This approach is comparable to a Matheuristic as described in Caserta and Voß (2010).

4.3 A Hybrid Algorithm

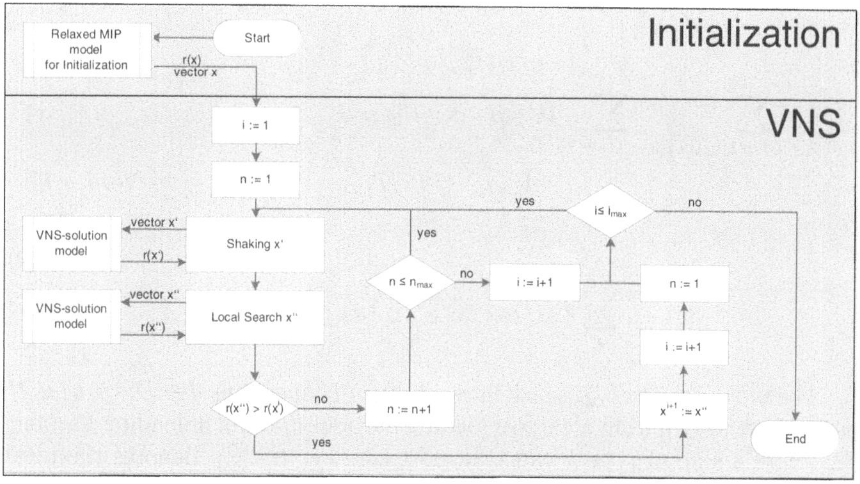

Figure 4.6: Visualisation of the Hybrid Algorithm

Due to the tremendous rise of the complexity of the problem size with increasing number of harbours, ships and cargo, real world problems with a large number of variables and constraints can not be solved within reasonable computational time with the original MIP model as described in the previous section (see Page 110 for an example of large size). To solve problems of realistic size, we designed a Matheuristic as shown in Figure 4.6. As initialization of the algorithm, the relaxed MIP model is solved and the first vector containing the harbour visiting sequence and the corresponding objective function value is obtained. This data is used as input for the following VNS. After each shaking procedure the newly constructed vector x' is transferred to our VNS-solution model, which in turn delivers the corresponding objective function values. This is done analogically for the local search procedure (x" respectively). The VNS process shown in Figure 4.6 corresponds to the pseudo code shown in Figure 4.8.

We will first describe the relaxed MIP model used for initialization before specifying the neighbourhoods we use for our VNS at the end of this section, which generates a solution of variables X_{ijdk}. The complete solution of the corresponding liner shipping network is constructed by the MIP model described in Section 4.2.2, where variables X_{ijdk} are fixed and all binary variables are relaxed. Only decision variables Z_{cdek}, that guarantee a cargo c is picked up at its loading harbour as well as dropped off at its unloading harbour, stay binary. In addition, to further limit the solution space, we define following cuts:

$$\begin{aligned} tijt_{cdek}^{v^{min}} \cdot Z_{cdek} - \sum_{(g,h,f)\in DirL_{cdekghf}} \sum_{v\in V/\{v^{min}\}} (tt_{ghfkv(1)} - tt_{ghfkv}) \\ \cdot V_{ghfkv} \leq TijT_{cdek} \qquad \forall c,d,e,k | \; ttt_{loadH_c,unloadH_c,e,k}^{min} < t_c^{max} \end{aligned} \tag{4.60}$$

$$\sum_{e} TijT_{cdek} \leq t_c^{max} \cdot Y_{cdk} \tag{4.61}$$

The index set $DirL_{cdekghf}$ defines all direct connections $d \in D$, $(g,h) \in H$ on the partial-trip from a cargo's loading harbour d_i to its unloading harbour d_j, where a ship of type k can transport cargo c. $tijt_{cdek}^{v^{min}}$ denotes the total travel time between the loading and unloading harbours of cargo c, for all four direction combinations, when travelling at slowest possible speed on a ship of type k.

Due to constraints (4.60) decision variable $TijT_{cdek}$ functions as a travel time limit for a ship of type k when transporting cargo c from its loading to its unloading harbour. Since the time for loading and unloading or the slack time in any harbour along the ship's round trip is not accounted for, $TijT_{cdek}$ can only be a lower bound for the complete round trip. With this lower bound on a cargo's total travel time, all possible ways of transportation of cargo c on a ship of type k exceeding the allowed maximum transportation time of cargo c (t_c^{max}), can be disregarded in the solution space as done in constraints (4.61). This allows us to find a very good initial solution within a short range of time (see Chapter 5).

This network design – containning the selected types of ships and harbours that these ships visit – is now transferred to our VNS. The VNS receives vectors of harbour visits for each type of ship. If a harbour is (not) visited, the vector has value 1 (0) at that position. The vectors for our example with 8 harbours have the fields 1 to 8 corresponding to harbours visited on the inbound trip and fields 9 to 14 representing harbours 7 to 2 on the outbound trip. The outermost harbours with index 1 and 8 do not have additional fields for the outbound part of a round trip. If the outermost harbours are visited, they have to be turning point harbours and therefore are called at on both, the inbound and outbound part of the round trip (see also Figure 4.7).

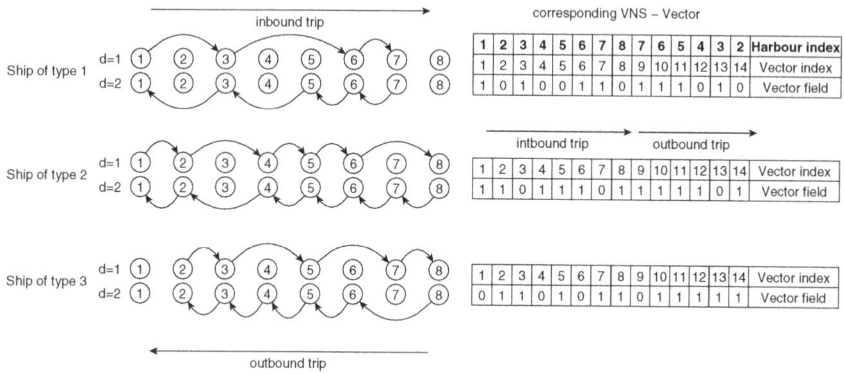

Figure 4.7: Vector setting example.

Similar to the VNS described by Mladenovic and Hansen (1997) and Hansen and Mladenovic (1997) the VNS in our case starts with the harbour visiting vector received from our initial solution (see pseudo code in Figure 4.8, step 1). To develop a valid solution for the visiting sequence we obtained from the initial solution, we solve our model, where all arcs the ships should travel on, are predefined and fixed (Variables X_{ijdk}). We will refer to this model as the VNS-solution model. This model differs from our initialization-model as decision variables $NShips_k$ now have to be integer again. The next while-loop (step 3 in VNS algorithm) is run, until an upper limit of iterations has been reached. Each of these iterations consists of setting the neighbourhood index to 1 and another while-loop (step 5 in VNS algorithm), which runs through a possible neighbourhood exchanges, unless the acceptance at the end breaks the while-loop. Inside this loop (step 6 in VNS algorithm), a shaking algorithm changes the vector settings. These changes have a greater effect on the solution value, than the following local search algorithm (step 7 in VNS algorithm), that only makes minor changes to the vector settings.

The acceptance criteria can stop the inner while-loop, if the solution value of the previous two shaking and local search solutions have led to a better solution than the best previous solution, either from the initial solution or the solution from the last inner while-loop. If none of the changes performed leads to a better solution than the previous solutions, the inner-loop iterator indicating the specific neighbourhood search is increased by one.

```
Step 1 Initialization: Get vector x of harbours visited by each type
   of ship from the relaxed, initialization model.
Step 2: Determine the initial solution value
Step 3: Set i := 1
Step 4: While iterator i ≤ i_max do
   Step 5: Set neighbourhood index n := 1
   Step 6: While n ≤ n_max do
      Step 7 Shaking: Randomly construct a harbour visiting vector
         x' ∈ V_n(x^i) for neighbourhood n and determine
         its solution value with the VNS-solution model.
      Step 8 Local search: Use a local search algorithm that is
         independent from all neighbourhood shaking algorithms. Again
         determine its solution value x'' with the VNS-solution model.
      Step 9 Acceptance: If r(x'') > r(x^i), then set x^{i+1} := x'';
         i := i + 1; and n := 1. Otherwise set n := n + 1
   End while
End while
```

Figure 4.8: The VNS Pseudo code

The three neighbourhoods we consider are created by a swap, an alternate and a relocate algorithm. The swap algorithm randomly selects two types of ships that exchange their vector settings at two randomly chosen harbours. Whenever a harbour is visited by a ship of type A and not visited by a ship of type B, type B visits that harbour after the swap exchange move and type A does not, and vice versa. If a harbour has not been visited by either types of ships, one of the randomly selected types of ships is forced to visit that harbour after the swap move. In our example with five harbours shown in Figure 4.9 (see network changes of swap move) a randomly selected harbour with index 4 (and 6 for the outbound part of the round trip) changes the vector settings of two randomly selected ship types (being 1 and 2 in our case). Harbour 4 which previously was not visited by a ship of type 1 is now visited on the inbound part of the round trip. After the swap move, harbour 4 (6 respectively) is therefore not visited on the outbound part of the round trip anymore. For all possible vector visiting states a corresponding swap move is given as shown in the harbour setting changes table of Figure 4.9. So for instance if both types of ships were visiting a selected harbour before the move, only one type of ship will stop at that harbour after the exchange.

With the alternate algorithm each type of ship will change the vector settings at the position of one randomly chosen harbour with the next type of ship, according to a predefined list of types of ships. The type of ship at the end of that list, exchanges its settings with the type of ship at the top of the list. Each type of ship exchanges its settings at a different randomly selected harbour. If there are more types of ships than harbours, different types of ships might change their vector setting at the position of the same harbour index. For the alternate harbour setting move and network changes to our example with five harbours see Figure 4.9.

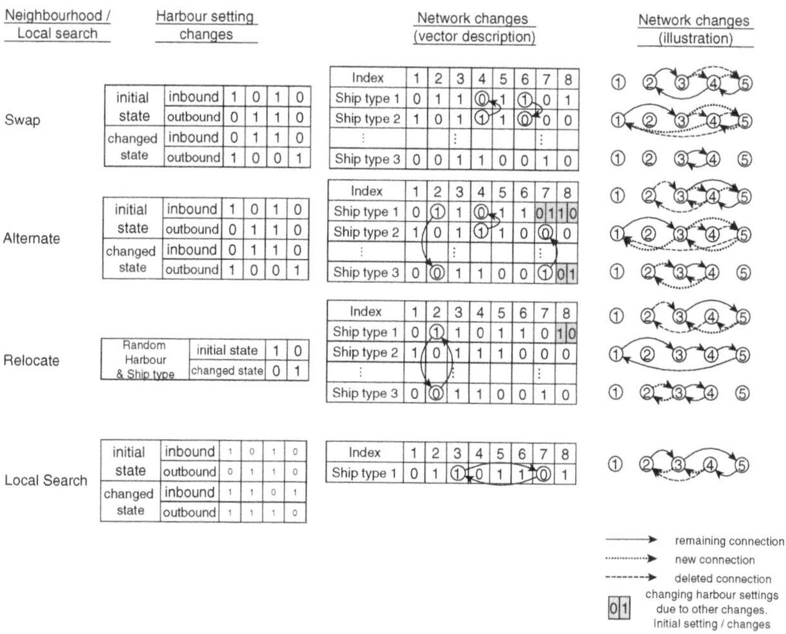

Figure 4.9: Neighbourhood and Local Search heuristics.

In difference to the swap algorithm, where the visiting sequence of a harbour is changed on either the inbound or outbound part of a ships' round trip, the relocate algorithm completely prohibits that a randomly chosen harbour is visited, when it was visited before the relocate move. For the relocation two types of ships are randomly chosen and exchange their vector settings at the position of one randomly selected visiting harbour. As shown in the harbour setting changes of the relocate move in Figure 4.9, a randomly selected harbour always changes the visiting state. If for example the harbour has been visited by both ship types, it will not be visited by these two ship types after the relocate move.

Our local search algorithm is a back-and-forth move where for each type of ship and each harbour the visiting status is changed. If a harbour for a specific type of ship is visited only on the inbound part and not on the outbound part of a round trip, the ship visits the harbour on its outbound part of the trip after the back-and-forth move has been completed. If one of these changes leads to a better solution value, the local search algorithm is finished. Again, please refer to Figure 4.9 for an example with five harbours.

Due to the very good solution quality we obtain by our initialization model the VNS finds better solution values within a couple of seconds.

Chapter 5

Computational Tests

The liner network design model and the Matheuristic used as solving algorithm presented in Chapter 4 will be tested on computational performance in the following. Furthermore, we will show adoptions to the liner network design according to seasons and environmental influences. In addition the influence of an additional kite propulsion system on the liner shipping network design will be analysed.

All tests were run on an eight thread Intel SMP 2.33 GHZ processor with 8 GB RAM, using Fico Xpress 7.1 parallel 64-bit. All eight processors are used by Fico Xpress to solve our relaxed mixed integer programming model. The VNS procedure is programmed in Java and is called upon in each optimisation step alternating with Fico Xpress. Therefore, only one of the 8 processors is in use for the Java program.

Section 5.1 describes how the test sets have been constructed and which data are used. The test results are evaluated in Subsection 5.2.1 – 5.2.3.

5.1 Generation of Test Data

As mentioned in Section 3.6 the test environment considers a maximum of 33 harbours: 10 harbours are allocated in the Gulf of Mexico, 16 harbours have a direct access to the North Atlantic, and 7 harbours are in the North Sea. For a detailed list of all harbours please turn to Table 3.3 on Page 65.

For each harbour to harbour relation 3 types of cargo exists. Each of these sets of cargo have a randomly assigned number of TEU, which is one of the following: 100, 110, 120, 130, 140, 150 or 160 TEU.

The revenue rev_c, measured in \$ per TEU, depends on the great circle distance D_c^{GC} between cargo c's loading and unloading harbour. The revenue linearly depends on the amount of nautical miles travelled and is obtained as follows:

$$rev_c = \frac{D_c^{GC}}{2} \tag{5.1}$$

This leads to a revenue of 0.5 \$ per nm and TEU. Container freight rates range from 1400\$ to 1800\$ per TEU for shipments between Europe and the US on pre financial level in 2008 (Beverelli et al. 2010, p. 10). As an example, the great circle distance between Le Havre and New York accounts to 3065nm. Multiplying this with 0.5 \$/nm and TEU, leads to a freight rate of 1532.5 \$/TEU, which falls into the range of 1400\$ and 1800\$ per TEU and therefore constitutes a good approximation. As a result, longer distances have higher freight rates and shorter distances lower freight rates, which reflects the charter rate structure as seen in real container shipping.

Each cargo is assigned a maximum allowed time for transportation (t_c^{max}). This will prevent a cargo to stay on board a ship too long and will guarantee a delivery within a reasonable time span. The maximum allowable travel time again depends on the great circle distance between a cargo's loading and unloading harbour and is calculated as follows:

$$t_c^{max} = \frac{D_c^{GC}}{5kn} \tag{5.2}$$

The maximum allowable transportation time is the fraction of the great circle distance from a cargo's loading and unloading harbour and an average allowed minimum transportation speed of 5 kn.

Six different types of ships that can either be equipped with or without an alternative sail propulsion system are assumed to be available for transportation. As shown in Tabel 5.1, the ships carrying capacity ranges between 4,100 TEU and 14,000 TEU.

Table 5.1: Ship data

Ship name	Container capacity [TEU]	Charter rate [US$/d]
Rafaela	4,100	23,000
Alicante	5,500	30,000
Moliere	6,550	35,000
Hamburg	8,580	45,000
Laetitia	9,661	51,000
Buenos Aires	14,000	72,000

The ships charter rates $charter_k$ are rounded inter- and extrapolated values received from Co (2011) and range between 32,000$ and 72,000$ per ship and day, depending on the ship's carrying capacity cap_k measured in TEU. The underlying function is formulated as follows:

$$charter_k = 4.9 \cdot cap_k + 3,377.4 \tag{5.3}$$

In a first step a maximum of 20 ships of each type is assumed to be available for the liner shipping network design.

The test sets used for evaluation of the liner service network design problem and algorithm are composed of eight varying parameters:

- Number of types of ships usable
- Number of harbours and regions considered
- Time of the year (seasons of the year)
- Fuel price
- Charter costs for different types of ships
- Revenue per TEU transported
- Maximum number of ships of each type
- Maximum time allowed for transporting a cargo from its loading to its unloading harbour

Seven different sets of available types of ships are constructed for the first parameter (see Table 5.2). The first two sets contain three types of ships with smaller carrying capacity, once with and once without an alternative kite propulsion system. These are compared with the two sets consisting of three types of ships with larger carrying capacity, again once with and once without an alternative kite propulsion. Additionally, the results of the set with all six types of ships are compared to their counterpart, a set with all ships including an alternative kite propulsion system. Last, a set with all six types of ships with and without alternative kite propulsion system installed, can be used in a mixed setting. The settings of the seven different sets of types of ships and their respective abbreviations are shown in Table 5.2.

The sets of harbours taken into account are composed according to the ocean or sea they access. For the following tests four different settings are considered. The first set consists of 16 harbours, lying on the coasts of

Table 5.2: Ship test settings

Abbreviation	Description	types of ships
3sSnS	3 small ships no sail	Rafaela, Alicante, Moliere
3sSwS	3 small ships with sail	Rafaela (w.s.)*, Alicante (w.s.), Moliere (w.s.)
3lSnS	3 large ships no sail	Hamburg, Laetitia, Buenos Aires
3lSwS	3 large ships with sail	Hamburg (w.s.), Laetitia (w.s.), Buenos Aires (w.s.)
6SnS	6 ships no sail	Rafaela, Alicante, Moliere, Hamburg, Laetitia, Buenos Aires
6SwS	6 ships with sail	Rafaela (w.s.), Alicante (w.s.), Moliere (w.s.), Hamburg (w.s.), Laetitia (w.s.), Buenos Aires (w.s.)
12S	12 ships	Rafaela, Rafaela (w.s.), Alicante, Alicante (w.s.), Moliere, Moliere (w.s.), Hamburg, Hamburg (w.s.), Laetitia, Laetitia (w.s.), Buenos Aires, Buenos Aires (w.s.)

(*w.s.: with sail)

the Atlantic Ocean. The second set is made up of those 16 harbours from the Atlantic Ocean region plus the seven harbours of the North Sea region, summing up to 23 harbours. The third set consists of 10 harbours in and around the Gulf of Mexico. The last set of harbours contains all 33 harbours (also see Table 3.3 on Page 65).

The influence of different weather conditions onto the network design according to the four seasons of a year is evaluated by taking the corresponding fuel consumption, travelled time and travelled distance values. This data is obtained from the computational tests of the environmental routing algorithms (see Chapter 3).

The default fuel price is assumed to be at 650$ per metric ton. Rising fuel prices have led ship owners to operate their ships in a slow or even super slow speed setting. Falling fuel prices and the resulting changes to the liner shipping network are also examined by reducing the fuel price to 500$/$mt$, a price paid for bunker fuel during the last financial crisis. Then an increased fuel price of 800$/$mt$ and its influence on the network design is also analysed.

Fuel prices, charter rates, revenue per transported TEU and maximum allowed transportation time of each cargo are the parameters, which are usually given externally due to the market situation. All other parameters like the number of tpyes of ships available, the maximum number of ships of each type of ship and the number of harbours and regions considered can be of great influence and have to be determined by the liner shipping company's top management.

The default charter rates are set as mentioned above (see Equation 5.3) and will be altered for different test sets. This is done by increasing the multiplier of Equation (5.3) from 4.9 to 7.5. This leads to charter rates from 34,127$ to 108,377$ per ship and day for 7.5 as the multiplier of Equation (5.3).

Market conditions greatly influence the revenue achieved, which can therefore be higher or lower than the default revenue calculated in Equation 5.1. Higher revenues are usually obtained on routes with a high transportation demand, e.g. container transport from Asia to Europe. Revenues might also be high, if the amount of free capacity on board of ships is scares due to a lack of appropriate ships. Economic downturns are often the cause for lower revenues, since less cargo needs to be transported and a surplus of free carrying capacity exists. Usually when this occurs, charter rates fall as well and shipowners begin to put ships out of service. To show the influence of changing revenue per cargo transported, the revenue per nm and TEU is increased and decreased from 0.5 to 0.6 and 0.4 respectively (also see Equation 5.1).

Changes in the network design due to a limited number of ships of each type will be shown by decreasing the maximum number of ships per type from 20 to 5.

If the maximum allowed transportation time for each cargo is high, a fleet of ships will most likely travel at the lowest reasonable speed. The opposite is the case for shorter maximum allowed transportation times and ships are forced to travel faster. In other words, if customers request a quicker delivery of their cargo, shippers might be forced to travel faster. To compare the influence of a lower maximum allowed transportation time of cargo, the average speed of transportation in Equation (5.2) is changed from 5kn to 15kn.

The VNS algorithm has a given maximum number of iterations before it is stopped. This is the test set's ninth parameter.

Test sets will be labelled by a ninefold sequence of parameter settings for identification (# harbours, # types of ships, season, fuel price, charter costs, Revenue \TEU, number of ships of each type, max transportation time, number of iterations). For example the parameter settings (16, 3lSnS, 02, 650, 4.9, 0.5, 7, 5, 20) represent a test set with the 16 harbours of the North Atlantic and the 3 larger ships Hamburg, Laetitia and Buenos Aires, that do not have an alternative kite propulsion system installed. They are operated during the second quarter of the year at a fuel price of 650\$/mt and charter costs that have been derived with a coefficient of 4.9 (see Equation 5.3). The revenue is calculated by 0.5\$ per *nm* and TEU and for each type of ship 7 ships are assumed to be available. The cargo has to be delivered with an average speed of 5kn and the VNS algorithm is stopped after 20 iterations.

5.2 Evaluation of the Test Results

5.2.1 Evaluation of Solution Approaches

The following test sets consist of different parameter settings and are compared with each other to evaluate the different results obtained. First the solution quality of the heuristic modelling approach is compared to the solutions obtained from the MIP model formulation. The results regarding objective function value and number of iterations of the Matheuristic is compared with the original MIP model for the example of different number of ships and type of ships travelling between the 10 harbours of the Gulf of Mexico in the first quarter of the year (see Table 5.3). The remaining parameters are set as follows: 650\$/mt fuel price, charter costs factor of 4.9, revenue of 0.5\$ per *nm* and TEU, 20 possible ships of one type, and cargo has to be delivered with an average speed of 5kn. Due to the increasing solution space with increasing number of harbours and ships and therefore resulting high computational times, a comparison of the Matheuristic solutions with solutions obtained from the original MIP model for large number of harbours and ships was not carried out. Only smaller test sets with 10 harbours and 3 to 6 types of ships are compared. Test sets with a higher number of ships and harbours either did not yield a feasible a solution for the original MIP model within reasonable time or the quality of the MIP solution remains unsatisfying due to a large optimality gap for a given time limit. As shown in Table 5.3 for test sets 6SnS and 6SwS the remaining gap of the MIP solution does not allow a comparison of the MIP objective function value with the heuristic objective function value.

The objective function values represent a weekly profit contribution for a liner shipping operator of shipping routes between harbours currently looked at. The profit is made up of the revenue earned for transporting cargo from its loading to its unloading harbour subtracted by fuel costs and ship type dependent charter rates. Other costs like maintenance costs, pilotage and harbour fees, overhead costs and salaries are not accounted for. For a practical use of this model all missing costs can easily be integrated.

Table 5.3: Comparison of solution quality between Matheuristic and the original mixed integer programming model

Test set	Heuristic / MIP	Objective function value	Number of iterations	Difference to MIP	MIP Gap
3sSnS	Heuristic	13,572,800	15	-4.73%	
3sSnS	Heuristic	14,435,000	25	1.32%	
3sSnS	MIP	14,246,874			19.11%
3sSwS	Heuristic	13,933,500	15	-3.6%	
3sSwS	Heuristic	16,026,400	25	10.87%	
3sSwS	MIP	14,455,188			17.23%
3lSnS	Heuristic	13,124,200	15	-2.58%	
3lSnS	Heuristic	14,640,600	25	8.67%	
3lSnS	MIP	13,472,123			23.07%
3lSwS	Heuristic	14,449,900	15	18.86%	
3lSwS	Heuristic	14.998.700	25	23.37%	
3lSwS	MIP	13,404,768			23.83%
6SnS	Heuristic	15,100,900	15		
6SnS	Heuristic	15,566,700	25		
6SnS	MIP	no solution obtained			
6SwS	Heuristic	15,517,800	15		
6SwS	Heuristic	16,872,200	25		
6SwS	MIP	no solution obtained			

The original MIP model is stopped for all test sets after 80,000s resulting in a remaining optimality gap as shown in the last column of Table 5.3. In order to receive solutions with an objective value close to the solution values of the original mixed integer model, the number of iterations has to be adjusted according to the number of harbours and ships considered. With increasing number of ships and harbours, the number of iterations of the VNS should be increased. For the test sets analysed here, we set the number of iterations to 15. This leads to solutions of appropriate quality while test sets with 25 iterations lead to higher objective function values than their MIP counterparts. The difference in the objective function value between two test sets with the same parameter setting but different number of iterations performed is given in the column labelled 'Difference to MIP' of Table 5.3. This difference is expresses as percentage of the objective function value for test sets solved by the Matheuristic divided by the objective function value of the same test set solved with the MIP model formulation (in percent - 100%). Note, a longer computational time for the strategic network design problem is still acceptable due to the relatively long planning horizon in relation to the time needed for computations. We can also see from Table 5.3 that the optimality gap of the test sets solved with the MIP model, increases with increasing sizes of ships. This can result from the higher degree of freedom with larger carrying capacity of the larger types of ships. For the test sets run with all six types of ships available, no solution could be obtained within 80.000s when solving the problem with the MIP model.

In order to show an objective function value for a large MIP model, the search for a test run with parameter settings (10, 3sSwS, 01, 650, 4.9, 0.5, 20, 5, 20) was stopped after 953,000 seconds with the best integer solution value found of 14,827,739 and a best bound of 16,895,524.28, still leaving an optimality gap of 13.95%.

Even though the VNS heuristic may stop in a local optimum, the best objective function value found so far has increases with additional number of iterations. Figure 5.1 shows a typical chart of objective function values over increasing number of iterations, which is similar for most of the other test sets. The first value of this chart is obtained from the initial, relaxed MIP model as described in Section 4.3 (see Page 98). Each of the following iterations consists of three shaking steps (see Section 4.3 on Page 100 for the three neighbourhoods swap, alternate and relocate) followed by a local search. The number of local searches accomplished, depends on the objective function value. If the objective function value obtained from the local search algorithm is improved compared with the preceding shaking algorithm, no further local searches are made and the Matheuristic proceeds with the next shaking algorithm. A maximum number of six local searches are completed if no better solutions can be obtained (see e.g. iteration 9 in Figure 5.1).

The objective function value tends to increase from the start until it gets close to an upper limit (see Figure 5.1). For this test set the upper limit seems to be close to 45 million$. Once being close to that upper limit the objective function value begins to vary and the difference in succeeding objective function values is higher again. For this test set this state is reached at iterations 6 or 7. The higher differences in succeeding objective function values for iterations 8 to 10 indicate that the VNS is not stuck in a local optimum. In some cases the objective function value drops to a lower level but increases to a new overall best solution (see end of iteration 7 to beginning

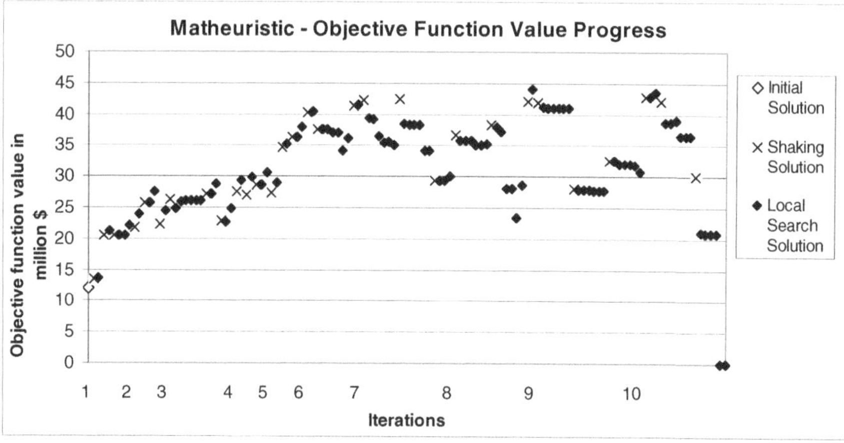

Figure 5.1: Progress of the objective function value during the Matheuristic run for test set (23, 3lSwS, 04, 650, 4.9, 0.5, 5, 5, 10).

of iteration 9 in Figure 5.1).

For networks with a larger number of harbours the results in Table 5.4 indicate that ships with a higher loading capacity should be used instead of ships with lesser carrying capacity (see for example test sets 3sSnS and 3sSwS compared to 3lSnS and 3lSwS). For test sets with larger ships the objective function value is significant higher compared to test set with the smaller type of ships. For the smaller network with only 10 harbours the three smaller types of ships with an installed kite system seem to be sufficient to serve that network at a higher objective function value than the three larger ships with a higher carrying capacity, which would operate at higher costs but cannot gain more profit, since cargo to be transported is limited.

5.2.2 Testing the Effect of a Kite Propulsion System

The test runs also show that the installation of a kite propulsion system has only a small effect on the objective function value. The difference in the objective function values between a test set with the same type of ships is given in the last column of Table 5.4. The percentage expresses the objective function value for test sets where ships have an alternative kite propulsion system installed divided by the objective function value of the same types of ships without a kite propulsion system (in percent -100%). Except for two couples of the test sets with 16 harbours, all other test sets show only a small difference when using or not using an alternative kite propulsion system. The

Table 5.4: Evaluating the effect of an alternative kite propulsion system

Test set	Number of Harbours	Available number of a given type of ship: Rafaela	Rafaela wS	Alicante	Alicante wS	Moliere	Moliere wS	Hamburg	Hamburg wS	Laetitia	Laetitia wS	Buenos Aires	Buenos Aires wS	Objective function value	Difference in objective function value
3sSnS	10	5		4		4								16,026,400	3.30%
3sSwS	10		5		4		4							16,572,800	
3lSnS	10							4		4		3		14,640,600	2.39%
3lSwS	10								4		4		4	14,998,700	
6SnS	10	3		4		4		3		3		2		15,100,900	2.69%
6SwS	10		2		3		3		4		2		3	15,517,800	
3sSnS	16	7		6		7								47,385,200	11.67%
3sSwS	16		7		7		7							53,644,800	
3lSnS	16							5		5		6		56,229,800	15.12%
3lSwS	16								6		8		6	66,242,800	
6SnS	16	8		7		7		6		4		4		63,718,200	1.15%
6SwS	16		8		5		6		7		6		4	64,461,800	
3sSnS	23	7		11		11								58,316,200	2.56%
3sSwS	23		8		11		10							59,848,300	
3lSnS	23							11		10		11		70,955,200	3.31%
3lSwS	23								11		11		10	73,386,000	
6SnS	23	10		11		9		9		8		8		93,760,100	3.45%
6SwS	23		9		11		9		11		7		8	97,107,200	
3sSnS	33	10		10		9								73,850,000	1.78%
3sSwS	33		10		8		10							75,187,600	
3lSnS	33							17		17		20		101,618,000	0.44%
3lSwS	33								16		18		12	102,068,000	
6SnS	33	7		8		5		12		11		7		119,137,000	0.51%
6SwS	33		6		8		5		13		10		8	119,748,000	

two couples of the test sets with 16 harbours are 3sSnS, 3sSwS and 3lSnS, 3lSwS. For these two the objective function value of ships travelling with an alternative kite propulsion system is 11.67% and 15.12% higher then their counterparts travelling without a kite propulsion system. The reason for this might be that weather and ocean currents conditions may have a greater influence on trips between these 16 harbours around the Antlantic Ocean than on trips conencting harbours of other regions. As an example, the difference in objective function value of 3.3% between the three small ships and 16 Harbours of the Atlantic Ocean, travelling either with or without an alternative kite propulsion, corresponds to an absolut difference of 546,400$ per week. Dividing this amount by 13, the total number of ships needed when using a kite propulsion, results in 42,031$ savings per week and installed kite system. If all kite related fixed and variable weekly costs exceed this amount, investing into a kite propulsion system is not profitable. It has to be kept in mind that a part or all of those differences in objective function values may result from using a heuristic solution approach, which does not guarantee finding an overall optimal solution.

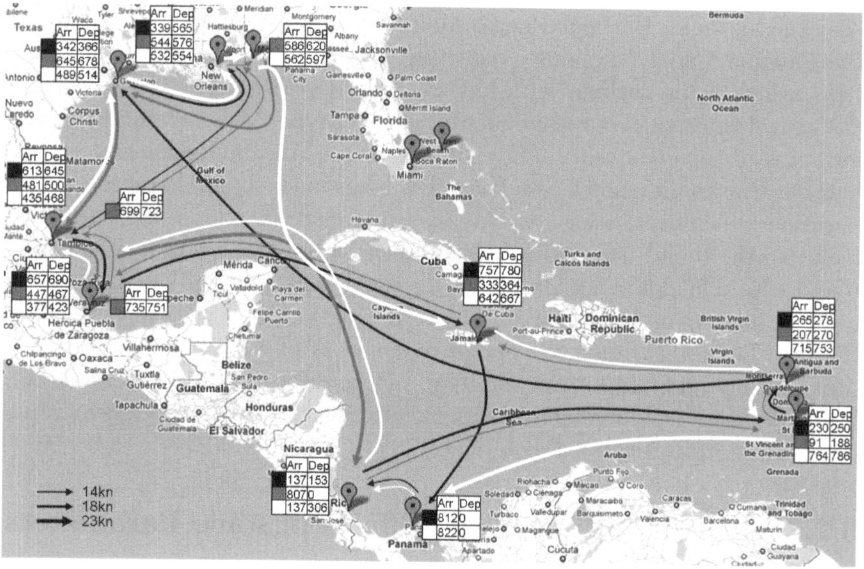

Figure 5.2: Harbour visiting sequence of ships of type 'Rafaela' (white line) 'Alicante' (grey line) and 'Moliere' (black line) and their corresponding schedules (see tables at harbours; Arr = arrival time; Dep = departure time)(©2011 Google). To view this figure in colour please refer to: www.springer-gabler.de/Buch/978-3-658-00698-3/A-Liner-Shipping-Network-Design.html.

Figure 5.2 shows a solution for the 3 smaller ships of type 'Rafaela', 'Alicante' and 'Molier' and harbours of the Gulf of Mexico. All three types of ships are in use. The black line indicates the round trip ship of type

'Moliere' is travelling on, the grey line represents the round trip of ship of type 'Alicante' and the white line corresponds to ship of type 'Rafaela'. The width of the lines indicates the speed at which a ship is travelling between two consecutive harbours. The smallest width corresponds to a speed of 14kn, the medium width to 18kn and the widest to 23kn. For example ships of type Moliere (black line) travelling at 14kn from New Orleans to Altamira, ships of type Alicante travelling at 18kn from Mobile to Houston and ships of type 'Rafaela' travelling at 23kn from Fort de France to Puerto Limon. With 5 ships of each type all available cargo can be transported between the harbours. The complete parameter setting of this underlying test set is (10, 3sSnS, 01, 650, 4.9, 0.5, 20, 5, 20) with an objective function value of 14,246,900$. Also given in the figure are the times when a ship will arrive in the next harbour. These times are presented in tables on the map located near the harbour. Harbour Puerto Moin located at the easterly entrance of the Panama Canal functions as starting and ending harbour of the round trips, which is the harbour with index 1. The departure time is set to 0 and the arrival time equals to 812 hours for ships of type 'Moliere' and 822 hours for ships of type 'Rafaela'. Only ships of type 'Alicante' start and end at harbour Puerto Limon in Costa Rica, which has index 2. The total round trip duration indicates that for a weekly visiting frequency 5 ships are needed to maintain the round trip. After 840 hours the ships start again for their next round trip. The differences in arrival and departure times at the harbours is used for loading or unloading activities. Longer harbour visits include times that can be used for maintenance or repair work or to catch up on possible delays. This additional stopover time might also be distributed among all harbours or adjusted manually by an operator according to unforeseen events or based on his operational experience.

5.2.3 Consideration of the Effects of some Parameters

Taking the above mentioned example and comparing it with a test set where the *speed* is not variable on each harbour to harbour trip but kept constant at an average speed of 18kn has an objective function value of 11,148,250$. This leads to the conclusion that the underlying model structure that allows varying speed settings on each leg of a round trip on its own leads to superior network designs improving the objective function value by 21.7% for the network considered. Installing a kite propulsion system might even further increase the objective function value.

The effect of *seasons* is not as significant as expected from the results of the operational computational tests from Section 3.6. There are small changes of networks constructed for equivalent parameter settings but different seasons. If these differences result from different seasons and their predominant weather, it will be difficult to prove. Changes seen from the results of the computational tests of the operational routing of Section 3.6 which depend on the direction of travel, might have been compensated by the round trip a ship performs. Ships travel in both directions, once with a reduced resistance and once with higher resistance. Fuel savings when travelling in one direction might then be compensated by a higher fuel consumption when travelling in the opposite direction.

Table 5.5: Evaluating the effect of changing fuel costs

			Available number of a given type of ship:													
Test set	Number of Harbours	Fuel costs [$]	Rafaela	Rafaela wS	Alicante	Alicante wS	Moliere	Moliere wS	Hamburg	Hamburg wS	Laetitia	Laetitia wS	Buenos Aires	Buenos Aires wS	Objective function value in thousands	Difference in objective function value
3sSnS	10	500	4		4		3								12,268	4.25%
3sSnS	10	800	5		4		4								11,747	
3sSnS	16	500	5		6		5								51,624	12.85%
3sSnS	16	800	6		7		7								44,988	
3sSnS	23	500	8		8		6								46,220	23.96%
3sSnS	23	800	10		11		9								35,144	
3sSnS	33	500	7		9		7								65,368	28.36%
3sSnS	33	800	11		13		10								46,827	
3sSwS	10	500		5		4		3							14,275	4.03%
3sSwS	10	800		6		4		4							13,699	
3sSwS	16	500		5		5		6							54,210	12.84%
3sSwS	16	800		7		7		7							47,248	
3sSwS	23	500		6		8		9							50,425	23.96%
3sSwS	23	800		8		11		11							38,342	
3sSwS	33	500		8		8		10							69,247	28.10%
3sSwS	33	800		10		12		13							49,786	
3lSnS	10	500							4		4		5		13,118	3.98%
3lSnS	10	800							4		5		6		12,596	
3lSnS	16	500							5		6		5		41,057	12.05%
3lSnS	16	800							6		7		7		36,111	
3lSnS	23	500							6		5		7		35,227	19.94%
3lSnS	23	800							9		8		11		28,202	
3lSnS	33	500							11		8		11		80,468	25.81%
3lSnS	33	800							14		11		15		59,697	
3lSwS	10	500								4		4		4	13,627	3.16%
3lSwS	10	800								5		5		4	13,196	
3lSwS	16	500								5		5		6	51,650	10.70%
3lSwS	16	800								7		7		7	46,125	
3lSwS	23	500								6		7		7	49,370	19.59%
3lSwS	23	800								8		9		9	39,697	
3lSwS	33	500								10		7		9	89,571	28.36%
3lSwS	33	800								11		12		13	64,165	
6SnS	10	500	2		3		4		3		2		2		14,836	4.03%
6SnS	10	800	2		3		3		4		3		4		14,238	
6SnS	16	500	5		3		4		4		4		3		53,912	12.60%
6SnS	16	800	4		4		4		5		5		6		47,116	
6SnS	23	500	7		7		6		5		6		7		74,940	22.47%
6SnS	23	800	6		8		9		7		8		9		58,103	
6SnS	33	500	10		7		9		7		7		6		103,141	26.78%
6SnS	33	800	7		8		11		7		12		9		75,516	
6SwS	10	500		2		3		3		3		4		3	15,380	3.67%
6SwS	10	800		2		4		3		3		4		4	14,816	
6SwS	16	500		4		4		4		4		5		4	57,706	11.39%
6SwS	16	800		5		4		6		5		5		4	51,133	
6SwS	23	500		6		5		6		6		7		6	83,093	20.92%
6SwS	23	800		6		7		8		7		6		5	65,708	
6SwS	33	500		4		3		3		3		4		3	109,972	26.24%
6SwS	33	800		6		4		7		7		7		7	81,113	

Changing the *fuel costs* has a significant influence on the solution value and the number of ships needed to maintain a promised liner service. As shown in Table 5.5 rising fuel costs from 500$ to 800$ per mt lower the objective function value when comparing test sets with the same parameter setting but only differing fuel costs. This relative effect is smaller for the test sets with a smaller number of harbours and increases with a higher number of harbours. Table 5.5 also shows that a larger number of ships of each type of ship is used for test sets with the higher fuel costs of 800$ per mt then their counterparts with only 500$ per mt. With a larger number of ships of each ship type each liner service has a longer round trip duration and therefore ships can travel at lower speed, which will reduce fuel consumption and therefore cut fuel costs. The amount of cargo transported and the structure of the underlying network is not changing much. The main difference between two test sets is only the decreasing profit margin with increasing fuel prices. The percentage in the last column of Table 5.5 is the difference in the objective function values for each test set pair. The percentage expresses the ratio of the objective function value (in percent -100%) of the test set with a fuel price of 800$ per mt divided by the solution value of its counterpart with a fuel price 0f 500$ per mt. All other test set parameters are set as follows: Season 2, charter rate coefficient 4.9, revenue coefficient 0.5, maximum naumber of ships of each type 20, number of iteration 25 and maximum allowed travel time obtained with a delivery speed of 5kn.

An *increasing charter rate* lowers the objective function value when comparing two test sets that only differ in the value of the charter rate coefficient. Other than with increasing fuel costs the number of ships of each ship type decreases or remains equally high (see Table 5.6). An overall decreasing number of ships can be seen for the larger test sets with 33 harbours. The structure of the network changes as well as the number of carried cargo. Not all cargo is worth to be transported at a higher given charter rate and therefore the number of harbour visits slightly decreases and fewer ships are needed. The differences in objective function values is greater for the larger test sets with 16 to 33 harbours than the differences for the smaller test sets with only 10 harbours. For these smaller test sets the difference stays below 8%. Again the percentage in the last column of Table 5.6 is the ratio of the objective function value (in percent -100%) for test sets with a higher charter rate to its counterpart with a lower charter rate. The parameter settings for the tests on changing charter rates are set to: Season 2, fuel price 500$ per mt, revenue coefficient 0.5, number of ships of each type available 20, maximum allowed delivery time for cargo obtained with 5kn and number of iterations set to 25.

The objective function value increases as expected with *increasing revenue*

Table 5.6: Evaluating the effect of changing charter rates

Test set	Number of Harbours	Charter rate coefficient	Available number of a given type of ship: Rafaela	Rafaela wS	Alicante	Alicante wS	Moliere	Moliere wS	Hamburg	Hamburg wS	Laetitia	Laetitia wS	Buenos Aires	Buenos Aires wS	Objective function value in thousands	Difference in objective function value
3sSnS	10	4.9	4		4		3								12,268	7.98%
3sSnS	10	7.5	3		4		4								11,289	
3sSnS	16	4.9	5		6		5								51,624	0.89%
3sSnS	16	7.5	5		6		5								51,164	
3sSnS	23	4.9	8		8		6								46,220	13.48%
3sSnS	23	7.5	6		7		8								39,990	
3sSnS	33	4.9	7		9		7								65,368	17.84%
3sSnS	33	7.5	7		9		7								53,705	
3sSwS	10	4.9		5		4		3							14,275	0.90%
3sSwS	10	7.5		4		4		4							14,146	
3sSwS	16	4.9		5		5		6							54,210	6.98%
3sSwS	16	7.5		6		5		5							50,426	
3sSwS	23	4.9		6		8		9							50,425	4.42%
3sSwS	23	7.5		6		7		8							48,194	
3sSwS	33	4.9		8		8		10							69,247	3.73%
3sSwS	33	7.5		8		8		8							66,664	
3lSnS	10	4.9							4		4		5		13,118	6.86%
3lSnS	10	7.5							4		4		3		12,218	
3lSnS	16	4.9							5		6		5		41,057	23.74%
3lSnS	16	7.5							6		5		5		31,310	
3lSnS	23	4.9							6		5		7		35,227	13.57%
3lSnS	23	7.5							5		6		7		30,445	
3lSnS	33	4.9							11		8		11		80,468	3.78%
3lSnS	33	7.5							11		7		10		77,426	
3lSwS	10	4.9								4		4		4	13,627	4.88%
3lSwS	10	7.5								3		5		4	12,961	
3lSwS	16	4.9								5		5		6	51,650	11.16%
3lSwS	16	7.5								4		5		6	45,885	
3lSwS	23	4.9								6		7		7	49,370	1.64%
3lSwS	23	7.5								5		7		8	48,562	
3lSwS	33	4.9								10		7		9	89,571	22.77%
3lSwS	33	7.5								8		9		8	69,173	
6SnS	10	4.9	2		3		4		3		2		2		14,836	2.64%
6SnS	10	7.5	3		3		2		3		3		2		14,445	
6SnS	16	4.9	5		3		4		4		4		3		53,912	9.55%
6SnS	16	7.5	4		4		5		3		5		2		48,764	
6SnS	23	4.9	7		7		6		5		6		7		74,940	4.31%
6SnS	23	7.5	6		8		6		6		5		6		71,713	
6SnS	33	4.9	10		7		9		7		7		6		103,141	25.83%
6SnS	33	7.5	7		6		6		7		9		1		76,499	
6SwS	10	4.9		2		3		3		3		4		3	15,380	3.54%
6SwS	10	7.5		3		3		3		3		3		3	14,834	
6SwS	16	4.9		4		4		4		4		5		4	57,706	2.42%
6SwS	16	7.5		4		3		5		4		3		4	56,310	
6SwS	23	4.9		6		5		6		6		7		6	83,093	31.05%
6SwS	23	7.5		4		5		6		6		5		5	57,292	
6SwS	33	4.9		4		3		3		3		4		3	109,972	23.32%
6SwS	33	7.5		3		4		4		3		3		3	84,327	

per TEU transported and constant fuel costs (see Table A.3 in Appendix A.5). The structure of the network only slightly changes when comparing the test sets with different revenues per TEU transported. For test sets with a larger number of harbours accounted for, a single harbour might be skipped on a round trip of one ship type compared to its counterpart with lesser or higher revenue per TEU. Especially for smaller test sets with only 10 harbours the only difference observable is that a harbour is for example visited on the outbound part of the round trip for the test set with the lesser revenue coefficient and on the inbound part of the round trip for the same type of ship in a test set with 0.6 as revenue coefficient.

For smaller test sets with only a few harbours to be visited, a smaller maximum *number of ships of each type* of ship does not lead to large differences in solutions values and to changing network structures. As soon as the number of harbours that could be visited on a round trip increases, a larger number of ships of a specific type of ship are in use if possible. The more ships available the more cargo can be picked up at their loading harbours and therefore the objective function value increases.

A smaller *maximum time* allowed for transporting a cargo from its loading to its unloading harbour leads to faster travelling ships. This constellation describes a situation that would occur when the market is asking for faster transportation of its cargo at the same freight rate. The structure of the networks with the same parameters setting except for the maximum allowed transportation time of cargo differs a lot. Not only the number of ships of each type in use changes but also the number and sequence of harbour visits of each type of ship on its round trip changes. There is no overall pattern observable that could describe the changes between each pair of test sets with differing maximum time allowed for transporting the cargo.

Chapter 6

Summary and Outlook

In this thesis a liner shipping network design is presented, which is for the first time capable of taking weather data such as wind and waves as well as currents into consideration. Additionally this model allows different speed settings between two consecutive harbours instead of an average assumed speed for a complete round trip. The use of a Matheuristic solution approach even finds solutions of good quality for large test scenarios or even real world problems of large size within reasonable time. This strategic network design problem is based on data obtained from an operational environmental routing algorithm. Here we apply a known shortest path algorithm to find the most fuel efficient path under time restriction. Now, in addition wind, waves and ocean currents and their interaction with a ship are accounted for. The ship behaviour under environmental influences and the resulting fuel consumption is based on an integrated, detailed ship model. This algorithm already satisfies fundamental requirements for practical use as a ship routing tool for trips between two harbours or any other two coordinates.

In Chapter 2 the reader is introduced to maritime transportation and especially to the problem of routing and scheduling of ships in different operating modes. Moreover, the main differences and special characteristics in routing and scheduling of ships compared to other vehicles like trains and trucks is emphasised.

One of the main issues of this thesis, the environmental routing, is investigated in Chapter 3. First, a literature review on this topic reveals a lack of research on weather dependent routing models. It is required as an underlying structure for the shortest path problem. Based on detailed weather data and a ship model, both also presented in this chapter, the SPP finds the most fuel efficient path between two harbours under given time constraints. Computational tests show that this Shortest Path algorithm provides better solutions than algorithms that do not account for influences from wind, waves and ocean currents. It turned out that the installation of an alternative kite propulsion system is not advisable in some cases. Savings from using a kite propulsion system are not significant in short sea shipping with short harbour to harbour distances and ships travelling along coasts. As shown, only on shipping routes across the North Atlantic the use of a kite propulsion system significantly reduces fuel consumption.

The other main issue of this thesis, the strategic liner network design, is subject of Chapter 4. A MIP model is formulated for the network design problem, which eliminates the lack of research found by an extensive literature review on this topic. The fundamental benefits form the network design presented in this thesis are the choice of speed on each trip between two consecutive harbours and the ability of solving large size problem instances. This ability originates from solving the problems with a Matheuristic. The combination of a VNS heuristic and a relaxed MIP model allows us to solve even large problem instances within reasonable time and a good solution quality.

The network design approach from Chapter 4 is evaluated by numerical tests in Chapter 5. The test set generation is described and the way of determining the parameters and their variation is provided. The testing results document that varying parameters like fuel costs, revenue and charter rates have changed the structure of a liner network whereas the season of the year and an alternative kite propulsion system do not have a significant effect on the network structure and overall objective function value in general. Only for some test instances where ships are travelling across the Atlantic Ocean larger improvements in the objective function values (>10%) have been notified (see Table 5.4 for test sets 3sS· · · , 3sS· · · and 16 harbours). The different types of ships used, a different number of harbours considered and a changing maximum allowed time for transporting cargo from its loading to its unloading harbour lead as expected to totally different network structures and solution values.

The comparison of our network design model with the possibility of variable speeds to test sets where the speed is not variable showed that our model leads to superior network designs. Installing a kite propulsion system might even further increase the objective function value.

Other ideas of application and improvements are to use this liner network design problem for fleet design or fleet deployment tasks where several different types of ships are compared to each other as alternative investments. The solution of the strategic network design model can then guide decision makers. Further research will include the possibility of transhipment of cargo between different types of ships and therefore different liner services. Transhipment will also allow to enlarge the model to develop feeder services where ships interact in a hub and spoke network configuration. Another characteristic of transportation via liner ships is the multi-commodity transport. Instead of transporting only one type of cargo different types are usually might be transported. Reefer containers for example could be an additional type of cargo, that have their own capacity restrictions and are transported at a different revenue level. Future model modifications might also include to account for harbour and canal restrictions such as limited draught which may also depend on tides.

Another topic for future research within the field of the strategic container liner service network design is allowing for different types of ships to operate on the same liner service. This will be useful when the required visiting frequency can only be met with more ships than the maximum number of a specific type of ships available. This will lead to a higher complexity when such additional model formulations are incorporated.

An approach always possible and highly recommended for the weather dependent network design is taking stochastic influences into account. Until now we only looked at average travel times, distances and fuel consumptions between two consecutive harbours of a round trip or liner service for each season of the year. For all data of each season and the 30 different starting times in any of these quarters of a year a stochastic distribution and all its parameters should be gathered. It might also have an influence on the outcome of the network design if the data are not calculated for starting times, that are evenly distributed within the season of the year, but rather letting the starting times being picked randomly within this quarter of the year. And last, another stochastic influence that should be accounted for is the amount of cargo being offered for transport in a specific harbour. This amount of cargo might as well depend on seasonal changes or of course fluctuate due to constantly changing market conditions.

When using the VNS or Matheuristic approach it is easily possible to deal with a liner shipping network alliance since the vectors transferred to the relaxed MIP model formulation are given as a fixed network design description. If the task would be to find a new network design for one of the partners of that alliance the network of the rest of the alliance can be given as a second given vector, that is stating, which types of ships are visiting which harbours along their round trip. But only the one vector representing the types of ships owned by a single liner company and its allocated harbour visits is then subject to change when performing a neighbourhood search or local search within the Variable Neighbourhood search procedure.

Appendix A

Appendix

A.1 Kite Propulsion Force Data Input

Table A.1: Data input for a kite of 160 m^2

Parameter	Value	Unit
a	50	
b	-40	
c	-10	
d	15	
γ_P	45°	
ρ_A	1.204	kg/m^3
A_D	160	m^2
c_W	0.5	

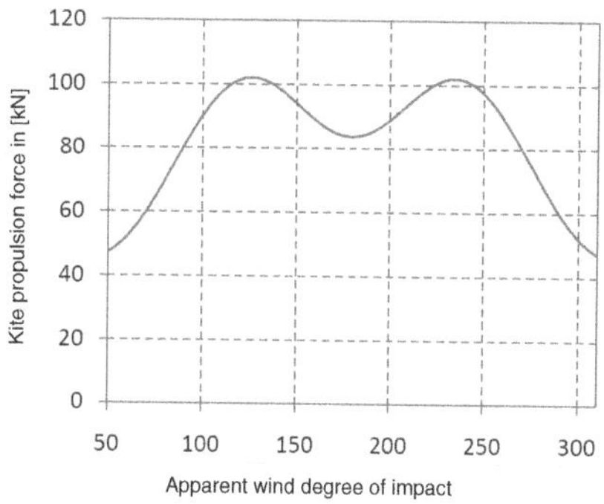

Figure A.1: Kite propulsion force gradient

A.2 Ship Data

Table A.2: Ship data

Ship name	Container capacity [TEU]	Length [m]	Breadth [m]	Height [m]	Draft [m]
Rafaela	4,100	281	32.3	20	12
Alicante	5,500	270.4	40	21.7	13.5
Moliere	6,550	300	40	24.2	14.5
Hamburg	8,580	334	42.8	24.8	14.61
Laetitia	9,661	350	42.8	27.3	15
Buenos Aires	14,000	365.5	51.2	29.2	16

Ship name	Breadth of cargo [m]	Depth of cargo [m]	Total height of cargo and ship above water [m]	Hull heigth above water [m]	Heigth of Cargo above water [m]
Rafaela	32.3	252.9	38.89	8	18.82
Alicante	40	243.36	40.59	8.2	18.82
Moliere	40	270	43.09	9.7	18.82
Hamburg	42.8	300.6	46.38	10.19	21.51
Laetitia	42.8	315	48.88	12.3	21.51
Buenos Aires	51.2	328.95	54.18	13.9	24.2

Ship name	Displacement [t]	Radius of gyration [ft]	Engine power [KW]	Consumption coefficient	Power coefficient
Rafaela	72,340	230.48	51,390	0.00028	0.895
Alicante	95,786	221.78	42,140	0.00031	0.886
Moliere	112,361	246.06	57,866	0.00026	0.794
Hamburg	128,445	273.95	72,240	0.00023	1.044
Laetitia	135,887	287.07	68,640	0.00024	1.053
Buenos Aires	171,866	299.79	72,240	0.00024	1.164

Ship name	Engine efficiency	Propulsion efficiency	Base consumption [mt/d]	Charter rate [US$/d]	Service speed [kn]
Rafaela	0.99	0.7	185.2	23,000	25.4
Alicante	0.99	0.7	152.9	30,000	23.2
Moliere	0.99	0.7	208.4	35,000	25.6
Hamburg	0.99	0.7	252.9	45,000	25.6
Laetitia	0.99	0.7	247.3	51,000	25.3
Buenos Aires	0.99	0.7	262.2	72,000	24.1

A.3 Wave Resistance Data Input

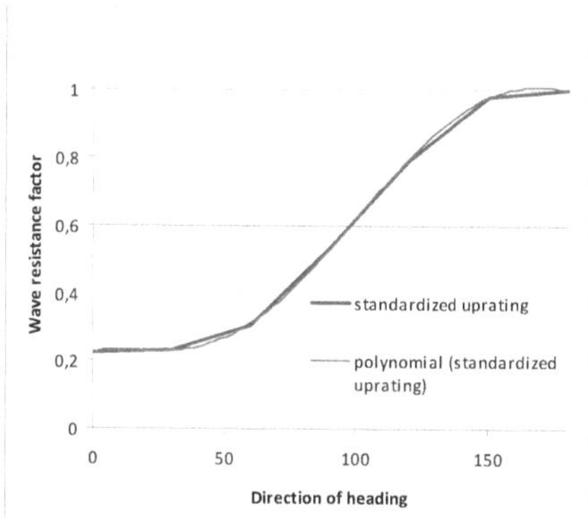

Figure A.2: Wave resistance factor according to (Yaozong 1989, p. 19-20)

A.4 Great Circle Navigation Formulas

We constructed our network similar to the way as Lee et al. (2002) described in his approach, in the following the generally known great circle navigation formulas that we applied in our Environmental-Routing algorithm are given. All values are in radians. A Course $C_{1,2}$ from a point 1 to any other point along a great circle route is obtained as follows:

$if((lon_1 - lon_2) < 0)then$

$C_{1,2} = \arccos\left(fracsin(Lat_2) - \sin(lat_1)\cos(D_{1,2})\text{sin}(D_{1,2}\cos(lat_1))\right)$

$else$

$C_{1,2} = 2\pi - \arccos\left(fracsin(Lat_2) - \sin(lat_1)\cos(D_{1,2})\text{sin}(D_{1,2}\cos(lat_1))\right)$

where $D_{1,2}$, the great circle distance between two point is calculated by the formulation.

$$D_{1,2} = \arccos\left(\sin(lat_1)sin(lat_2) + cos(lat_1)cos(lat_2)\cos(lon_2 - lon_1)\right)$$

Figure A.3: Determination of a great circle route

A.5 Computational Tests - Changing Revenue

Table A.3: Evaluating the effect of changing revenues

Test set	Number of Harbours	Revenue coefficient	Available number of a given type of ship: Rafaela	Rafaela wS	Alicante	Alicante wS	Moliere	Moliere wS	Hamburg	Hamburg wS	Laetitia	Laetitia wS	Buenos Aires	Buenos Aires wS	Objective function value in thousands
3sSnS	10	0.4		3		4		5							11,026
3sSnS	10	0.5		4		4		3							13,934
3sSnS	10	0.6		3		4		5							17,722
3sSnS	16	0.4		5		5		5							40,942
3sSnS	16	0.5		5		5		5							50,531
3sSnS	16	0.6		5		5		5							57,205
3sSnS	23	0.4		5		5		5							34,525
3sSnS	23	0.5		5		5		5							40,070
3sSnS	23	0.6		5		5		5							55,560
3sSnS	33	0.4		5		5		5							35,571
3sSnS	33	0.5		5		5		5							47,399
3sSnS	33	0.6		5		5		5							54,103
3sSwS	10	0.4	4		3		4								11,782
3sSwS	10	0.5	4		4		3								14,435
3sSwS	10	0.6	4		4		4								18,153
3sSwS	16	0.4	5		5		5								42,341
3sSwS	16	0.5	5		5		5								52,010
3sSwS	16	0.6	5		5		5								64,089
3sSwS	23	0.4	5		5		5								37,490
3sSwS	23	0.5	5		5		5								45,680
3sSwS	23	0.6	5		5		5								56,170
3sSwS	33	0.4	5		5		5								42,392
3sSwS	33	0.5	5		5		5								51,074
3sSwS	33	0.6	5		5		5								64,470
3lSwS	10	0.4							2		5		4		11,962
3lSwS	10	0.5							4		4		3		14,450
3lSwS	10	0.6							5		4		4		18,533
3lSwS	16	0.4							5		5		5		41,389
3lSwS	16	0.5							5		5		5		61,644
3lSwS	16	0.6							5		5		5		63,589
3lSwS	23	0.4							5		5		5		45,587
3lSwS	23	0.5							5		5		5		54,586
3lSwS	23	0.6							5		5		5		63,391
3lSwS	33	0.4							5		5		5		37,643
3lSwS	33	0.5							5		5		5		46,051
3lSwS	33	0.6							5		5		5		51,701
3lSnS	10	0.4								4		4		4	11,242
3lSnS	10	0.5								5		4		2	14,442
3lSnS	10	0.6								4		3		4	17,242
3lSnS	16	0.4								5		5		5	38,904
3lSnS	16	0.5								5		5		5	59,704
3lSnS	16	0.6								5		5		5	61,895
3lSnS	23	0.4								5		5		5	41,117
3lSnS	23	0.5								5		5		5	43,992
3lSnS	23	0.6								5		5		5	61,515
3lSnS	33	0.4								5		5		5	33,778
3lSnS	33	0.5								5		5		5	45,723
3lSnS	33	0.6								5		5		5	51,063

Parameter settings: Season 4, fuel price 650$ per mt, charter rate coefficient 4.9, number of ships of each type available 5, maximum allowed delivery time for cargo obtained with 5kn and number of iterations set to 25

Bibliography

Aas, B.; Gribkovskaia, I.; Halskau Sr, Ø.; Shiopak, A. (2007) *Routing of supply vessels to petroleum installations*, International Journal of Physical Distribution & Logistics Management, vol. 37, no. 2, 164–179

Agarwal, R.; Ergun, O. (2008) *Ship Scheduling and Network Design for Cargo Routing in Liner Shipping*, Transportation Science, vol. 42, no. 2, 175–196

Agarwal, R.; Ergun, O. (2010) *Network Design and Allocation Mechanisms for Carrier Alliances in Liner Shipping*, Operations Research, vol. 58, no. 6, 1726–1742

Ahuja, R. K.; Magnanti, T. L.; Orlin, J. B. (1993) *Network Flows: Theory, Algorithms, and Applications*, Prentice Hall, 1st ed.

Al-Khayyal, F.; Hwang, S.-J. (2007) *Inventory constrained maritime routing and scheduling for multi-commodity liquid bulk, Part I: Applications and model*, European Journal of Operational Research, vol. 176, no. 1, 106–130

Allsopp, T.; Mason, A.; Philpott, A. (2000) *Optimising Yacht Routes under Uncertainty*, in: *Proceedings of the 2000 Fall National Conference of the Operations Research Society of Japan, Tokyo*, 176–183

Ang, J. S. K.; Cao, C.; Ye, H.-Q. (2007) *Model and algorithms for multi-period sea cargo mix problem*, European Journal of Operational Research, vol. 180, no. 3, 1381–1393

Appelgren, L. H. (1969) *A Column Generation Algorithm for a Ship Scheduling Problem.*, Transportation Science, vol. 3, no. 1, 53–68

Asariotis, R.; Benamara, H.; Hoffmann, J.; Misovicova, M.; Nez, E.; Premti, A.; Sitorus, B.; Valentine, V.; Viohl, B. (2011) *Review of Maritime Transport 2010*, United Nations Conference on Trade and Development

Azaron, A.; Kianfar, F. (2003) *Dynamic shortest path in stochastic dynamic networks: Ship routing problem*, European Journal of Operational Research, vol. 144, no. 1, 138–156

Barnhart, C.; Kniker, T. S.; Lohatepanont, M. (2002) *Itinerary-Based Airline Fleet Assignment.*, Transportation Science, vol. 36, no. 2, 199–217

Barnhart, C.; Schneur, R. R. (1996) *Air Network Design for Express Shipment Service*, Operations Research, vol. 44, no. 6, 852–863

Bellman, R. E. (1957) *Dynamic Programming*, Princeton University Press

Bendall, H. B.; Stent, A. F. (2001) *A Scheduling Model for a High Speed Containership Service: A Hub and Spoke Short-Sea Application*, International Journal of Maritime Economics, vol. 3, no. 3, 262–277

Beverelli, C.; Benamara, H.; Asariotis, R. (2010) *Oil Prices and Maritime Freight Rates: An Empirical Investigation*, URL `http://www.unctad.org/en/docs/dtltlb20092_en.pdf`, accessed on 27.01.11

Bilgen, B.; Ozkarahan, I. (2007) *A mixed-integer linear programming model for bulk grain blending and shipping*, International Journal of Production Economics, vol. 107, no. 2, 555–571

Brønmo, G.; Christiansen, M.; Nygreen, B. (2007) *Ship routing and scheduling with flexible cargo sizes*, Journal of the Operational Research Society, vol. 58, no. 9, 1167–1177

Brown, G. G.; Graves, G. W.; Ronen, D. (1987) *Scheduling Ocean Transporation of Crude Oil*, Management Science, vol. 33, no. 3, 335–346

Brown, G. G.; Kline, J. E.; Rosenthal, R. E.; Washburn, A. R. (2007) *Steaming on Convex Hulls*, Interfaces, vol. 37, no. 4, 342–352

Bunkerworld (2011) *Bunker prices*, URL `http://www.bunkerworld.com/prices/port/nl/rtm/?grade=IFO380`, accessed on 17.08.11

BWI (2011) *Bunkerworld Index*, URL `http://www.bunkerworld.com/prices/index/bwi`, accessed on 12.10.11

Cariou, P. (2011) *Is slow steaming a sustainable means of reducing CO_2 emissions from container shipping*, Transportation Research: Part D, vol. 16, no. 3, 260–264

Caserta, M.; Voß, S. (2010) *A Math-Heuristic Algorithm for the DNA Sequencing Problem*, in: C. Blum; R. Battiti (Eds.) *Learning and Intelligent Optimization, Lecture Notes in Computer Science*, vol. 6073, Springer Berlin / Heidelberg, 25–36

CGM, C. (2011) *Lines Services - French Asia Line 12*, URL http://www.cma-cgm.com/eBusiness/Schedules/LineServices/ServiceSheet.aspx?ServiceCode=JEX, accessed on 27.04.11

Chen, H. H. (1978) *A dynamic program for minimum cost ship routing under uncertainty*, Ph.D. thesis, Massachusetts Institute of Technology

Cho, S.-C.and Perakis, A. N. (1996) *Optimal liner fleet routeing strategies*, Maritime Policy & Management, vol. 23, no. 3, 249–259

Christiansen, M. (1999) *Decomposition of a Combined Inventory and Time Constrained Ship Routing Problem*, Transportation Science, vol. 33, no. 1, 3–16

Christiansen, M.; Fagerholt, K.; Nygreen, B.; Ronen, D. (2007) *Chapter 4 Maritime Transportation*, in: C. Barnhart; G. Laporte (Eds.) *Transportation, Handbooks in Operations Research and Management Science*, vol. 14, Elsevier, 189–284

Christiansen, M.; Fagerholt, K.; Ronen, D. (2004) *Ship Routing and Scheduling: Status and Perspectives*, Transportation Science, vol. 38, no. 1, 1–18

Co, H. P. . (2011) *Harpex, Container Ship Chart Rates*, URL http://www.harperpetersen.com/harpex/harpexRH.do?timePeriod=Months6&&dataType=Harpex&dataType=TEU700&floatLeft=None&floatRight=None, accessed on 03.04.11

Conference, I. T. T. (2008) *The Seakeeping Committee Final report and recommendations to the 25th ITTC*

Cordeau, J.-F.; Toth, P.; Vigo, D. (1998) *A Survey of Optimization Models for Train Routing and Scheduling*, Transportation Science, vol. 32, no. 4, 380–404

Crainic, T. (2003) *Long-Haul Freight Transportation*, in: F. S. Hillier; R. W. Hall (Eds.) *Handbook of Transportation Science, International Series in Operations Research & Management Science*, vol. 56, Springer US, 451–516

Crainic, T.; Kim, K. (2007) *Handbook of Transportation Science*, chap. Intermodal Transportation, North-Holland, Amsterdam, 467–537

Crainic, T. G. (2000) *Service network design in freight transportation*, European Journal of Operational Research, vol. 122, no. 2, 272–288

Danckwardt, E. C. M. (1969) *Ermittlung des Widerstandes von Frachtschiffen und Hecktrawlern beim Entwurf*, Schiffbauforschung, vol. 8, 3/4, 124–160

Dantzig, G.; Fulkerson, R.; Johnson, S. (1954) *Solution of a Large-Scale Traveling-Salesman Problem*, Journal of the Operations Research Society of America, vol. 2, no. 4, 393–410

Dantzig, G.; Ramser, J. (1959) *The truck dispatching problem*, Management Science, vol. 6, no. 1, 80–91

Desrosiers, J.; Pelletier, P.; Soumis, F. (1983) *Plus court chemin avec contraintes d'horaires*, RAIRO - Recherche oprationnelle, vol. 17, no. 4, 357–377

Desrosiers, J.; Soumis, F.; Desrochers, M. (1984) *Routing with time windows by column generation*, Networks, vol. 14, 545–565

Dijkstra, E. W. (1959) *A Note on Two Problems in Connexion with Graphs*, Numerische Mathematik, vol. 1, 269–271

Dong, J.-X.; Song, D.-P. (2012) *Quantifying the impact of inland transport times on container fleet sizing in liner shipping services with uncertainties*, OR Spectrum, vol. 34, 155–180

Enercon (2010) *Segelrotor-Schiff E-Ship 1 in der Erprobung*, Windblatt Enercon Magazin, 6

Fagerholt, K. (1999) *Optimal fleet design in a ship routing problem*, International Transactions in Operational Research, vol. 6, no. 5, 453–464

Fagerholt, K. (2004) *Designing optimal routes in a liner shipping problem*, Maritime Policy & Management, vol. 31, no. 4, 259–268

Fagerholt, K.; Heimdal, S. I.; Loktu, A. (2000) *Shortest Path in the Presence of Obstacles: An Application to Ocean Shipping*, The Journal of the Operational Research Society, vol. 51, 683–688

Fagerholt, K.; Johnsen, T. A. V.; Lindstad, H. (2009) *Fleet deployment in liner shipping: a case study*, Maritime Policy & Management, vol. 36, no. 5, 397–409

Fagerholt, K.; Laporte, G.; Norstad, I. (2010) *Reducing fuel emissions by optimizing speed on shipping routes*, Journal of the Operational Research Society, vol. 61, no. 3, 523–529

Farvolden, J. M.; Powell, W. B. (1994) *Subgradient Methods for the Service Network Design Problem*, Transportation Science, vol. 28, no. 3, 256–272

Fisher, M. L.; Rosenwein, M. B. (1989) *An interactive optimization system for bulk-cargo ship scheduling*, Naval Research Logistics, vol. 36, 27–42

Gavish, B.; Graves, S. C. (1978) *The Travelling Salesman Problem and Related Problems*, Operations Research Center Working Paper

Gribkovskaia, I.; Laporte, G.; Shiopak, A. (2008) *A tabu search heuristic for a routing problem arising in servicing of offshore oil and gas platforms*, Journal of the Operational Research Society, vol. 59, no. 11, 1449–1459

Grønhaug, R.; Christiansen, M.; Desaulniers, G.; Desrosiers, J. (2010) *A Branch-and-Price Method for a Liquefied Natural Gas Inventory Routing Problem*, Transportation Science, vol. 44, no. 3, 400–415

Grünert, T.; Irnich, S. (2005) *Optimierung im Transport 2: Wege und Touren*, Berichte aus der Informatik, Shaker

Hagiwara, H. (1989) *Weather routing of (sail-assisted) motor vessels*, Ph.D. thesis, TU Delft

Hansen, P.; Mladenovic, N. (1997) *Variable neighborhood search for the p-median*, Location Science, vol. 5, no. 4, 207–226

Hapag-Lloyd (2011) *Services from Asia nach North America*, URL `http://www.hapag-lloyd.de/de`, access on 27.04.11

Hoffmann, J. (2008) *The modal split of international goods transport*, UNCTAD Transport Newsletter, vol. 38, 14–16

Horie, K. (2011) *Suntory Mermaid II*, URL `http://www2.suntory-mermaid2.com/english/index.html`, accessed on 22.04.11

Hughes, G. (1957) *Skin Friction and Turbulence Stimulation, Formal Discussion*, in: M. L. Acevedo (Ed.) *8th International Towing Tank Conference*, 220

Imai, A.; Shintani, K.; Papadimitriou, S. (2009) *Multi-port vs. Hub-and-Spoke port calls by containerships*, Transportation Research: Part E, vol. 45, no. 5, 740 – 757

Irnich, S.; Desaulniers, G. (2005) *Shortest Path Problems with Resource Constraints*, in: G. Desaulniers; J. Desrosiers; M. M. Solomon (Eds.) *Column Generation*, Springer US, 33–65

ISL (2011a) *Shipping Statistics Yearbook 2010*

ISL (2011b) *World Container and General Cargo Shipping*, Shipping Statistics and Market Review (SSMR), vol. 55, no. 5/6

James, R. (1957) *Application of Wave Forecasts to Marine Navigation*, Ph.D. thesis, New York University

Kang, J.; Kim, Y. (2002) *Stowage planning in maritime container transportation*, Journal of the Operational Research Society, vol. 53, no. 4, 415–426

Karlaftis, M. G.; Kepaptsoglou, K.; Sambracos, E. (2009) *Containership routing with time deadlines and simultaneous deliveries and pick-ups*, Transportation Research: Part E, vol. 45, no. 1, 210–221

Kjeldsen, K. H. (2009) *Liner shipping network design, routing and scheduling*, Ph.D. thesis, CORAL - ASB

Kopf (2011) *Alstersonne*, URL `http://www.kopf-solarschiff.de/`, accessed on 22.04.11

Korsvik, J. E.; Fagerholt, K.; Laporte, G. (2011) *A large neighbourhood search heuristic for ship routing and scheduling with split loads.*, Computers & Operations Research, vol. 38, no. 2, 474–483

Korsvik, J. R.; Fagerholt, K.; Laporte, G. (2010) *A tabu search heuristic for ship routing and scheduling*, Journal of the Operational Research Society, vol. 61, no. 4, 594–603

Kranke, A. (2009) *Neu Basisdaten für die Seeschifffahrt*, Verkehrs Rundschau, vol. 45, 36–39

Kreitner, J. (1939) *Heave, Pitch and Resistance of Ship in a Seaway*, TINA

Lai, M. F.; Lo, H. K. (2004) *Ferry service network design: optimal fleet size, routing, and scheduling*, Transportation Research Part A: Policy and Practice, vol. 38, no. 4, 305–328

Langevin, A.; Soumis, F.; Desrosiers, J. (1990) *Classification of travelling salesman problem formulations*, Operations Research Letters, vol. 9, no. 2, 127–132

Laporte, G. (2009) *Fifty Years of Vehicle Routing*, Transportation Science, vol. 43, no. 4, 408–416

Laporte, G. (2010) *A concise guide to the Traveling Salesman Problem*, Journal of the Operational Research Society, vol. 61, no. 1, 35–40

Lawrence, S. A. (1972) *The years ahead*, Lexington, Mass., Lexington Books

Lee, H.; Kong, G.; Kim, S.; Kim, C.; Lee, J. (2002) *Optimum Ship Routing and It's Implementation on the Web*, in: W. Chang (Ed.) *Advanced Internet Services and Applications*, *Lecture Notes in Computer Science*, vol. 2402, Springer Berlin / Heidelberg, 11–34

Lin, D.-Y.; Liu, H.-Y. (2011) *Combined ship allocation, routing and freight assignment in tramp shipping*, Transportation Research: Part E, vol. 47, no. 4, 414–431

Lo, H. K.; McCord, M. R. (1998) *Adaptive ship routing through stochastic ocean currents: general formulations and empirical results*, Transportation Research Part A: Policy and Practice, vol. 32, 547–561

Maersk (2011) *Atlantic: North America - Europe, Mediterranean, Middle East and Indian Subcontinent*, URL `http://www.maerskline.com/link/?page=brochure&path=/routemaps/newnetwork/MEIS`, accessed on 27.04.11

McCord, M. R.; Lee, Y.-K.; Lo, H. K. (1999) *Ship Routing through Altimetry-Derived Ocean Currents*, Transportation Science, vol. 33, no. 1, 49–67

Meng, Q.; Wang, T. (2010) *A chance constrained programming model for short-term liner ship fleet planning problems*, Maritime Policy & Management, vol. 37, no. 4, 329–346

Meng, Q.; Wang, T. (2011) *A scenario-based dynamic programming model for multi-period liner ship fleet planning*, Transportation Research: Part E, vol. 47, no. 4, 401–413

Miller, C. E.; Tucker, A. W.; Zemlin, R. A. (1960) *Integer Programming Formulation of Traveling Salesman Problems*, J. ACM, vol. 7, no. 4, 326–329

Mladenovic, N.; Hansen, P. (1997) *Variable neighborhood search*, Computers & Operations Research, vol. 24, no. 11, 1097–1100

Montes, A. A. (2005) *Network Shortest Path Application for Optimum Track Ship Routing*, Master's thesis, Naval Postgraduate School

Moor, D.; Murdy, D. (1968) *Motions and Propulsion of Single Screw Models in Head Seas*, London: Royal Institution of Naval Architects, 403–445

Nachmani, G. (2007) *Minimum-Enery Flight Path for UAVS using Mesocale Wind Frocasts and approximate Dynamic Programming*, Master's thesis, Naval Postgraduate School

Nishimura, E.; Imai, A.; Janssens, G. K.; Papadimitriou, S. (2009) *Container storage and transshipment marine terminals*, Transportation Research: Part E, vol. 45, no. 5, 771–786

Norstad, I.; Fagerholt, K.; Laporte, G. (2011) *Tramp ship routing and scheduling with speed optimization*, Transportation Research: Part C, vol. 19, no. 5, 853–865

Notteboom, T. E.; Vernimmen, B. (2009) *The effect of high fuel costs on liner service configuration in container shipping*, Journal of Transport Geography, vol. 17, no. 5, 325–337

NYK (2009) *NYK and Nippon Oil Corporation Joint Project Auriga Leader Completes Seven Months of Voyages Using Solar Power*, URL `http://www.nyk.com/english/release/31/NE_090908.html`, accessed on 22.04.11

Padhy, C. P.; Sen, D.; Bhaskaran, P. K. (2008) *Application of wave model for weather routing of ships in the North Indian Ocean*, Natural Hazards, vol. 44, 373–385

Papadakis, N, A.; Perakis, A, N. (1990) *Deterministic minimal Time Vessel Routing*, Operations Research, vol. 38, no. 3, 426–438

Perakis, A. N.; Jaramillo, D. I. (1991) *Fleet deployment optimization for liner shipping Part 1. Background, problem formulation and solution approaches*, Maritime Policy & Management, vol. 18, 183–200

Perakis, A. N.; Papadakis, N. A. (1989) *Minimal Time Vessel Routing in a Time-Dependent Environment*, Transportation Science, vol. 23, no. 4, 266–276

PlanetSolar (2011) *PlanetSolar*, URL `http://www.planetsolar.org/de/home.html`, accessed on 22.04.11

Rana, K.; Vickson, R. G. (1991) *Routing Container Ships Using Lagrangean Relaxation and Decomposition*, Transportation Science, vol. 25, no. 3, 201–214

Ronen, D. (1983) *Cargo ships routing and scheduling: Survey of models and problems*, European Journal of Operational Research, vol. 12, no. 2, 119–126

Ronen, D. (1986) *Short-Term Scheduling of Vessels for Shipping Bulk or Semi-Bulk Commodities Originating in a single Area*, Operations Research, vol. 34, 164–173

Ronen, D. (1993) *Ship scheduling: The last decade*, European Journal of Operational Research, vol. 71, no. 3, 325–333

Ronen, D. (2011) *The effect of oil price on containership speed and fleet size*, Journal of the Operational Research Society, vol. 62, no. 1, 211–216

Rosmorduc, V.; Mertz, F.; Guinehut, S. (2011) *WP 04-Global MFC-PI GLO-CLS-Toulouse-FR Product User Manual*, Internet, URL `ftp://ftpsedr.cls.fr/pub/myocean_v1/MYO-WP4-PU-CLS-PUM-Armor3D-V1Str1.pdf`, accessed on 22.06.11

Schneekluth, H. (1988) *Hydromechanik zum Schiffsentwurf*, Koehler

Schneekluth, H.; Betram, V. (1998) *Ship Design for Efficiency and Economy*, Butterworth-Heinemann, Oxford, 2nd ed.

Schönknecht, A. (2007) *Entwicklung eines Modells zur Kosten- und Leistungsbewertung von Containerschiffen in intermodalen Transportketten*, Ph.D. thesis, Technische Universität Hamburg-Harburg

Shintani, K.; Imai, A.; Nishimura, E.; Papadimitriou, S. (2007) *The container shipping network design problem with empty container repositioning*, Transportation Research Part E: Logistics and Transportation Review, vol. 43, no. 1, 39–59

Sigurd, M. M.; Ulstein, N. L.; Nygreen, B.; Ryan, D. M. (2005) *Ship Scheduling with Recurring Visits and Visit Separation Requirements*, in: *Column Generation*, Springer, 225–245

SkySails (2009) *Die SkySails Technologie*, URL http://www.skysails.info/deutsch/produkte/die-skysails-technologie/, accessed on 15.09.11

SkySails (2011) *SkySails*, URL http://www.skysails.info/, accessed on 23.02.11

Stopford, M. (2009) *Maritime Economics*, Routeledge

Szlapczynska, J.; Smierzchalski, R. (2007) *Adopted isochrone Method Improving Ship Safety in Weather Routing with Evolutionary Approach*, International Journal of Reliability, Quality & Safety Engineering, vol. 14, no. 6, 635–645

Tchibo (2009) *Sustainable Development Report*, URL http://www.tchibo-nachhaltigkeit.de/controller.aspx?n=120&l=2, accessed on 23.02.11

Tiedemann, J. (2011) *Chart of the week*, Alphaliner weekly Newsletter, vol. 14, 1

Wang, D. Z. W.; Lo, H. K. (2008) *Multi-fleet ferry service network design with passenger preferences for differential services*, Transportation Research Part B: Methodological, vol. 42, no. 9, 798–822

Wilson, I.; Roach, P. (2000) *Container stowage planning: a methodology for generating computerised solutions*, Journal of the Operational Research Society, vol. 51, no. 11, 1248–1255

Yan, S.; Chen, H. L. (2002) *A scheduling model and a solution algorithm for inter-city bus carriers*, Transportation Research Part A: Policy and Practice, vol. 36, no. 9, 805–825

Yan, S.; Tseng, C.-H. (2002) *A passenger demand model for airline flight scheduling and fleet routing*, Computers & Operations Research, vol. 29, no. 11, 1559–1581

Yaozong, Z. (1989) *Bestimmung der im Seegang zusätzlich erforderlichen Antriebsleistung von Schiffen*, Schriftenreihe Schiffbau. Hamburg: Universität Hamburg - Institut für Schiffbau

The manufacturer's authorised representative in the EU is Springer Nature Customer Service Centre GmbH, Europaplatz 3, 69115 Heidelberg, Germany. If you have any concerns regarding our products, please contact ProductSafety@springernature.com

Printed and bound by CPI Group (UK) Ltd, Croydon, CR0 4YY
25/09/2026
02222895-0003